The Ultimate Guide to Business Process Management

Everything You Need To Know
and How to Apply It to Your Organization

Theodore Panagacos

www.ultimateguidetobpm.com

Cover design by Vanessa No Heart. Visit her amazing portfolio at:
www.vanessanoheart.net

"Drive thy business or it will drive thee."

- Benjamin Franklin

CONTENTS

ACKNOWLEDGMENTS

The methodologies, concepts, frameworks, and historical information within this book have been collated from publicly available open source information as well as industry best-practice standards. I would like to thank both Clinton Thomson from Accenture Management Consulting Group and Vikas Gubbi from Monash University Business School for their important contributions to *The Ultimate Guide to Business Process Management*. Both Clinton and Vikas worked with several organizations to test all the information in this book and ensure its concepts and methodologies could be practically implemented and achieve the intended benefits.

Chapter 1

INTRODUCTION

Why is it that some organizations seem to adapt effortlessly to evolving market conditions, whereas others miserably fail? How many times has an organization attempted to improve a process in one area, only to find that it has caused a whole host of problems in another? Worse yet, why are organizations still wasting millions of dollars trying to fix these problems?

It's questions like these that I was confronted with when I first started my career as a junior business graduate. Perhaps like you, I was frustrated by how inefficient and unnecessarily complex some organizations were—particularly when it was obvious they didn't have to be. I found that many organizations (particularly those that have been in existence for twenty years or more) were poorly structured, used limiting processes, and invested in expensive technologies that were constraining their ability to function rather than enabling it. Unfortunately, these problems are still very much relevant to 90 percent of global organizations today.

There are numerous reasons why organizations don't operate efficiently. Some business analysts may argue that innovative technologies (such as smart phones) have allowed consumers to be more demanding of the services they receive. Others will argue that changes to legislative requirements (such as the Sarbanes-Oxley Act) have placed tighter controls on organizations and therefore hampered their freedom to operate in a more flexible manner.

While both of these justifications may hold merit, it is no secret that the key to a successful organization is entirely dependent on how it is structured in the first place. If an organization has a well-defined foundation, then it will not matter if consumers change their buying habits or new technologies are introduced. As long as an organization has a simple framework that identifies people, process, governance, and technology, then it will always have the ability to adapt and improve efficiency regardless of what external conditions it faces.

John Zachman, a founder of the Enterprise Architecture discipline, always describes business design as being similar to the way an industrial architect designs a building. He says one must always pour the foundation before laying down the first, second, and third floors. However, many organizations choose to do this in reverse. They attempt to build the second and first floors before pouring the foundation—the result being a very shaky structure that will inevitably collapse.

Hence lies the reason for this book—*The Ultimate Guide to Business Process Management*. A few years ago, I realized there were few management books available that actually described how to build, identify, and manage processes within an organization. Even today, if you perform a search on Amazon.com or Google, you will only find a handful of publications that depict the proper method for building a BPM capability within an organization. And even at the time of writing this book, the entry under *Business Process Management* on Wikipedia is still largely incorrect.

The following are additional problems I discovered in my research:

- Most published books on BPM contain incorrect information.

- Many books focus on a very specific theme within the BPM discipline (e.g., process modeling).

- Some books have been written from a purely academic perspective or written for a non-business audience.

- Some books claim to discuss BPM, but subsequently describe everything *except* the application of process management.

Even more alarming, one book claimed to be a beginner's guide to BPM, but then went on to solely focus on IT investment. No wonder so many people are confused!

Rest assured that if you're after the single source of truth for BPM, then you've definitely come to the right place. I'm assuming that by holding this book in your hands (or e-reader), you want to know everything about BPM in a single, convenient, business-focused book. Alternatively, you could have been delegated by a manager to implement BPM in your workplace, but you're a little unsure of where to start. If so, then this book is perfect for you too.

Regardless, I'd like to think this book has been written for people of all backgrounds and all levels with an organization. I would be the first to admit that when I started my career, the concept of BPM was very confusing. Everyone I spoke to and every publication I read would gravitate towards explaining the use of other change management functions such as Six Sigma or Lean Manufacturing. While these functions are useful in the right environment, they don't exactly cover the entire spectrum of the BPM discipline.

The good news is that BPM is neither a hard function to understand, nor is it difficult to implement. This book will explain the step-by-step details on how to improve your culture, enforce governance and standards, and invest in the right technologies to help manage your business more effectively. At the end of the book, I would expect you to be able to walk into any organization, large or small, and be able to quickly assess its efficiency by querying its structure and the method used to deliver its products or services.

Either way, I want to congratulate you on the purchase of this book. You've made a great investment in both yourself and your knowledge of the change management industry. *The Ultimate Guide to Business Process Management* was written to cover every aspect of BPM and provide you with the right detail to successfully apply its frameworks within any organization.

Now let's get started…

Chapter 2

OVERVIEW OF
BUSINESS PROCESS MANAGEMENT

What you will learn in this section:

- What is Business Process Management (BPM)

- Why BPM is required

- How the discipline of BPM evolved

- The benefits of BPM

- Critical success factors for implementing BPM

- Pitfalls to avoid in implementing BPM

The Definition of BPM

Imagine you've walked into a café early in the morning, desperately needing a cup of coffee to kick start your day. You walk in, order your coffee, find a seat, and wait for the barista to serve your coffee to you at your table. The process sounds pretty simple, right? Well, next time you walk into a café, have a look at the entire process from beginning to end.

From the time you order your coffee to the time it's given to you at your table, approximately thirty to forty processes have taken place. This might seem like a lot; but if you consider the steps it takes for the barista to process your order, make the coffee, and serve you, then you'll realize a significant number of processes need to take place. The actual process of making the coffee is significant in itself. The barista needs to boil the water, clean the pipes of the coffee machine, boil the milk to the right temperature, add the sugar, etc. Depending on what you've ordered, a cup of coffee could take up to twenty processes to make—particularly if you've ordered those delicious ones that include cream and flavored syrup.

Essentially, this is what Business Process Management (BPM) is all about. Next time you're at a café observing its processes, have a look to see if any processes could be improved to speed up delivery time and reduce cost. Peer closely at how many steps it takes to process an order at the cash register, then examine the process used to actually make the cup of coffee. If you can identify at least two unnecessary processes, then you're on your way to becoming a certified process analyst. As an example, does the barista really need to hand your coffee to another employee before it's served? Or, are they able to hand it to you directly over the counter?

Everything we do in our daily life has a process associated with it. Starting your car, before driving to work in the morning, is a process. Cleaning the dishes after dinner is also a process. In a business context, BPM is no different. Each business activity has a specific set of processes to support its execution. When you undertake a particular task, you knowingly or unknowingly follow a process. These processes usually involve interaction between work, people, and technology. Therefore, as an employee, it's very important to understand the principle and execution techniques that help define processes. Doing so opens up the ability to improve effectiveness, efficiency, and productivity.

The next logical step here is to ask, how can these business processes be managed? The answer is simply the adoption of BPM.

Taking the café example into consideration, BPM is the science of building, identifying, and managing processes so they can be improved for maximum efficiency. BPM deals with identifying all the processes associated with your organization; analyzing them for efficiency and effectiveness; measuring the results over a period of time; and optimizing these processes. BPM is solely concerned with continuously improving the way work gets done, in order to make the process more efficient, less costly, and more productive for your organization.

Academically, BPM has been defined in a variety of ways. Perhaps the best definition I've come across was by Paul Harmon of Business Process Trends. He defined BPM as, " a management discipline focused on improving corporate performance by managing a company's business processes." He further elaborated that BPM is a holistic management approach that aims to align business processes with changing business needs by continuously focusing on optimizing them.

Why BPM?

Before we begin to dive deeper into the discipline of BPM, it's first important to discuss *why* its adoption is so important for an organization. This is perhaps the most fundamental problem that confronts the BPM community today. Many process analysts still struggle to convince others of the merits of using such a discipline.

In complex business environments, BPM offers a standard and scalable solution for managing processes. These solutions include person-to-person work steps, system-to-system communications, or combinations of both. It integrates various independent disciplines of process modeling, process simulation, workflow, process execution, process monitoring, Enterprise Architecture, Lean, and Six Sigma into one unified standard to manage change.

As shown in Figure 1, BPM is a comprehensive discipline that allows organizations to design, model, deploy, and manage business processes as per changing market dynamics. It creates actionable business intelligence in real time and helps organizations to rapidly respond to change.

Figure 1

As shown in Figure 1, BPM provides organizations with the most comprehensive ability to document, assess, and improve the enterprise.

- **Function analysis** is used to assess the functions performed by an organization at the macro level. This identifies growth opportunities and provides guidance for strategic planning.

- **Service analysis** is used to identify manual processes for automation and helps prepare them for integration with IT platforms.

- **Process analysis** is an assessment of end-to-end processes that aids process analysts to identify process improvements and optimize business performance.

- **Information analysis** is used to define and assess the flow of information between various stakeholders, identify any gaps, and optimize those channels.

- **Workflow analysis** is used to define and assess data workflow between applications, networks, and systems.

In this book, I am going to focus on the function of process analysis. The reason for this focus is because the other functions are typically performed by IT specialists and business architects. However, process analysis is performed by *process analysts* and their role is by far the most important in an organization's BPM capability.

The following table illustrates some key drivers for adopting BPM from the perspective of the key stakeholders of an organization—enterprise, management, employees, and customers.

Stakeholders	Key drivers for adopting BPM
Enterprise	- Requirement for processes and tools to support organic and inorganic growth such as new product launches, company mergers, and acquisitions, etc. - Changes in organizational structure, both strategic and operational - Change in business strategy - Legal compliance or regulation—for example, Sarbanes Oxley requirements; ISO requirements, etc. - Need for business agility to respond to market opportunities and threats
Management	- Need for reducing the "go to market" time - Improvement or development of a reliable performance measurement system - Development of end-to-end visibility of processes - Need for centralization of process controls - Need for process standardization to reduce duplication and unnecessary effort - Need for ability to produce more from less, especially in tough economic times
Employees	- Improvement of low employee motivation due to duplicate processes resulting in efforts being spent on unnecessary tasks - Encouragement for improvement of employee skills - Need for optimizing individual productivity - Need for an increase in employee empowerment - Clarification of an employee's role and responsibilities - Provision for clear communications and understanding of the process between employees

Customers/ suppliers/ partners	<ul><li>Improvement of service quality to customers</li><li>Improvement of lead delivery time</li><li>Rate increase for "get it right first time"</li><li>Reduction of high costs associated with the processes which ultimately result in savings for the customer</li></ul>

Table 1

The Evolution of BPM

At the time this book was written, there was no definitive consensus within the BPM community as to when humans began depicting processes and managing them. However, it has been argued that the Egyptians adopted some form of primitive workflow system that was used for building and engineering purposes (the most recognized was means used to build the pyramids). However, in more modern times, there is certainly little argument as to when process management became a mainstream discipline.

After the conclusion of World War II, many of the industrialized nations moved to rebuild themselves after their economies and resources were ravaged by the need to support the war. These countries (specifically the United States, Germany, Japan, and the United Kingdom) focused on manufacturing. During this time, organizations became savvier about implementing ways to streamline production and reduce waste.

From the late 1950s to early 1960s, manufacturing companies began to adopt more standardized means to analyze processes in the form of time and motion. Essentially, these efforts focused on statistical measurements that were aimed at reducing the total time associated with a particular process. The focus for many organizations also trended towards training workers to follow specific, repetitive steps that ensured consistent quality of product as well as shorter production time.

From the 1970s onwards process management methodologies and frameworks evolved continuously through innovation, customization, increased customer focus, and business growth. However, with the introduction of computers and automated technologies in the early 1970s, the rate of this evolution became rapid. Looking back on this history, we now acknowledge that the evolution of BPM can be depicted in five distinct phases as shown in Figure 2 below.

Evolution of Business Process Management

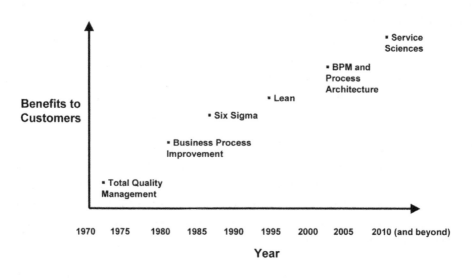

Figure 2

Total Quality Management (TQM) and Just in Time (JIT) tools initiated the first phase of process management. During the late 1940s, consumers in the United States perceived that Japanese products were of poor quality and cheaply made. Japan's industrial leaders recognized this as a problem and subsequently invited quality experts, such as Edward Deming and Joseph Juran, to learn how to achieve total quality in a mass production organization. Following the advice provided by experts like Deming and Juran, TQM became widely adopted by major Japanese companies in the 1980s and 1990s.

TQM was a discipline that was used by organizations to provide customers with the exact products and services that met their needs. The cultural aspects with the organization required quality in all phases of the company's operations, with the view that processes be performed right the first time and, therefore, defects and waste eradicated from operations. The two key objectives of TQM were for an organization to achieve 100 percent customer satisfaction and zero percent defects.

Companies who have implemented TQM include Ford Motor Company, Phillips Semiconductor, Motorola, and the Toyota Motor Company. The benefits these companies claimed from the adoption of TQM are:

- Process efficiency leading to improved profit per product or service by elimination of unnecessary steps and wasteful expenditure at the operations level

- Elimination of repairs and reworks

- Reduced warranty and customer support costs

JIT is the predecessor of TQM, but was not as widely adopted during the first phase of BPM's evolution. Many Japanese manufacturing organizations adopted JIT-practice in the 1970s. JIT was first developed and perfected by Toyota. Elements of JIT ensured that raw materials arrived at the production facility only when they were actually needed. By saving inventory costs, organizations were able to lower unit costs. Ultimately, customers paid less money for the cost of products.

The second phase of process management (still used today) surfaced during the late 1980s when the focus shifted from TQM to Business Process Improvement concepts. Many organizations assessed there was a critical need to manage the statistical data from TQM processes. This realization forced organizations to start questioning the *reason* behind the need to complete a process, as opposed to *how* to execute it more efficiently. James Harrington, who wrote several books on this subject, is credited with pioneering the Business Process Improvement concept. He went on to develop several methodologies around time measurement and benchmarking.

Today, the term Business Process Improvement is rarely used and has been replaced by the generic term "BPM." Next time you're at a conference or workshop and someone mentions Business Process Improvement, you will now know that they likely studied BPM during the late 1980s and early 1990s. Those individuals are also probably aware of the historical evolution of the discipline.

The Six Sigma concept forms the third phase of the BPM evolution. Bill Smith at Motorola conceptualized it in 1986, but Six Sigma gained rapid momentum in the early 1990s when it showed success in large organizations such as General Electric (GE) and Sony. GE started their Six Sigma program in 1994 under the leadership of Jack Welch. Within five years of starting the program, GE reported $2 billion worth of savings that stemmed directly from the Six Sigma initiative.

Six Sigma is a set of practices developed to improve processes by methodically eliminating defects. A defect is defined as the nonconformity of a product or service, and the Six Sigma Defect is defined as anything outside of customer specification. Six Sigma's key units of measurement are Defects Per Unit (DPU) and Defects Per Million Opportunities (DPMO). Processes that operate with Six Sigma levels of quality produce 3.4 defects per (one) million opportunities.

Earlier programs, such as TQM, produced improvements through quality, but had no visible impact on an organization's net income. The goal of Six Sigma is not only to achieve Six Sigma levels of quality, but also to improve the organization's profitability.

Lean philosophy gained major notoriety, along with the publicity of Six Sigma, and forms the fourth phase of the BPM evolution. It was widely used in the mid-1990s by Toyota, Boeing, McDonalds, Intel, and Hewlett Packard. Lean manufacturing is a generic process management philosophy derived mostly from the Toyota Production System. Lean uses a set of tools that assists in the identification and steady elimination of waste in a process by using the least amount of human effort, least amount of investment in tools, and the least engineering time to develop a new product. Examples of tools used in Lean manufacturing are Value Stream Mapping, FiveS, Kanban (pull system) and Poka-Yoke (error proofing).

As we move further into the twenty-first century, the next potential evolution for BPM is Service Sciences. This discipline advocates the ability for an organization to align itself and its processes exactly to customer expectations instead of the producing a predetermined set of products and services. Service Sciences aims to link corporate objectives and goals to every individual component of the enterprise, and it ensures that the business can meet customer expectations every time regardless of what they request. For example, rather than just producing cars in high volumes, Service Science advocates that a car will not be built *unless* a customer has specifically ordered it—and that it has been ordered based on their exact specifications.

The Benefits of BPM

As more and more organizations transform themselves into customer focused, process-centric organizations, the adoption of BPM will naturally gain more popularity. The principle value proposition of BPM was, and is, its ability to help organizations process more services and products with less effort, higher quality and at a reduced cost. Typically, BPM focuses on three core benefits—efficiency, effectiveness, and agility.

A study conducted by Gartner in 2008 found that by implementing BPM, 78 percent of organizations received a 15 percent or higher return on investment than those that did not have a BPM capability. And apart from the direct financial benefits, it was also found that these organizations were successful in reducing errors, improving their service levels and increasing the transparency of their business processes.

As shown in Figure 3 below, while the initial benefits associated with BPM are in the form of lower operating costs, the more an organization implements BPM standards the more strategic benefits it can realize.

Benefits from BPM Implementation

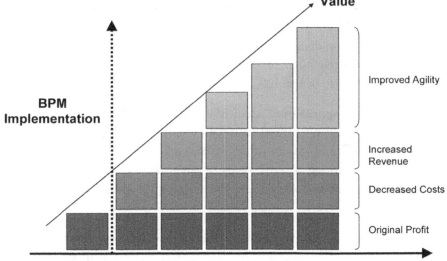

Figure 3

At a holistic level, BPM offers the following suite of benefits to the organization:

1) **BPM saves an organization's time and money:** BPM helps to identify redundant processes and eliminate duplication of work tasks. By standardizing business processes, organizations are able to reduce their operating costs by executing repeatable process that achieve the

same result every single time. And processes that are standardized become stronger candidates for automation. This helps reduce the work turnover cycle by reducing waste, enhancing efficiency and ultimately boost profitability.

2) **Improved business agility:** BPM enhances an organization's ability to sense potential opportunities or threats and help prioritize its response strategy. By adopting BPM, organizations have the ability to sustain volatile economic conditions by adding or removing services that can be differentiated between "desirable" and "essential." It also allows organizations to go to market with new products more quickly. Improved business agility provides visibility, control, and flexibility to respond better to customer's needs and expectations.

3) **Enhanced business intelligence:** With effective recording and monitoring of business processes, BPM offers the ability to track and locate essential information and produce reports for senior management that provide insight into the performance of those processes. BPM facilitates the dissemination of information in a timely manner, thus improving reliability of the information necessary to make judicious time-sensitive decisions.

4) **Improved operational accountability:** BPM provides high accountability to all departments within an organization by providing the ability to track and monitor budgets and deliverables. Documentation of business process activity helps organizations to achieve a system of checks and balances, thereby minimizing the potential for fraud, errors or loss.

5) **Continuous improvement:** BPM creates an environment for continuous process improvement in an organization and facilitates its ability to implement those improvements. It also helps to automate processes through technology that almost always results in significant cost savings. Automation reduces manual work, decreases lead times, and increases straight-through-processing rates. In this context, it's important to note that successful organizations with a BPM capability are usually seen to gradually phase out disparate legacy systems.

6) **Good compliance and regulatory governance:** In today's business environment there are a wide array of government rules and regulations which organizations need to follow. Successful BPM implementation

strives to achieve effective, coherent controls in place and at every process level. It involves tools, procedures, policies, and business metrics across the company so there is always "one version of the truth." This helps the organization keep track of their obligations, and ensure they are compliant with applicable standards. By having clearly defined processes, BPM provides the ability to avoid potentially costly repercussions of non-compliance.

7) **Effective measurement:** Computer science engineer Tom De Marco once said "you can't control what you can't measure". BPM strives to quantify the outcomes of operational activities—cost, throughput, cycle time, quality, customer satisfaction, or any other output—using measurement tools (such as Lean and Six Sigma). Effective measurement closes the feedback loop in the process management cycle, and provides managers with crucial information they can leverage to make further improvements.

8) **Effective risk management:** Good risk management is an integral component of any process. In BPM, documented processes are reviewed and assessed by process analysts from a risk perspective whereby effective controls are embedded in all processes and for all levels of staff. Process analysts are able to greatly reduce the overall risk to an organization by enforcing rigorous process management in all business units.

9) **Effective operational management**: Organizations that have successfully implemented BPM usually witness operational efficiency through shorter cycle times, lower costs, and the ability to handle additional work with no linear increase in staff. This results from process improvement and prevents lapses with former unproductive methods or practices. By having an effective process management system in place, business leaders can maintain a comprehensive understanding of their own processes, measure them effectively, and make sound decisions on how to move their businesses forward.

10) **Performance visibility**: BPM enhances the end-to-end visibility of a process that makes it performance transparent to those staff members who are responsible for it. By monitoring the performance of a process, a staff member can react accordingly and remediate any waste or problems in a much quicker fashion. BPM provides the means to

conduct performance measurement across an organization and can display the results in management dashboards. Process analysts can investigate further to isolate the root causes of bottlenecks such as time delays and high processing costs.

Critical Success Factors

Implementing BPM can be a comprehensive project that spreads across both functional and organizational boundaries. It impacts all stakeholders of an organization including clients, consultants, vendors and business partners. As a result, stakeholder relationships need to be managed as a part of any BPM implementation project. While each implementation project is unique, I have identified some critical success factors that you should consider as you deploy BPM throughout your organization:

1) **Development of your BPM Strategy:** This is the starting point for any BPM implementation. Having a BPM strategy that completely aligns with the organization's business goals is the first and most critical success factor. The strategy should be written so that it contains a structured and systematic approach to the implementation of a BPM capability. It needs to include a detailed business case that shows the difference between the current approach the organization uses and the benefits realized if BPM is adopted. The BPM strategy should also define a delivery framework which first focuses on relatively simple, achievable projects that also have a clear business benefit. However, the best thing of all is that this book has already done most of the hard work for you. The BPM implementation approach described in this book will provide you with the relevant information you need to build your own strategy and business case and will minimize the need to start completely from scratch.

2) **Stakeholder's commitment and empowerment:** Executive sponsorship is an absolute "must have" prior to implementing a BPM strategy. It is crucial that higher management (specifically the CEO or COO) gives their required attention, support, funding, commitment and time in order for the organization to reap the true benefits from BPM. This commitment also helps overcome various political hurdles that can be anticipated during BPM implementation. Further, commitment from middle management is also critical as some staff may experience a change in roles and responsibilities in light of new or improved

processes. This may involve scrutiny of staff performance through process measurement, tracking, and capacity planning. It is important that as soon as the processes, people roles, structure and people performance measurements and feedback systems have been redesigned and implemented, employees should be trusted and empowered to perform their tasks. Quite often it is seen that if key managers are not sufficiently involved, they may not buy in to the redesigned processes for a number of reasons (usually out of fear of losing their jobs). Management should aim to create the right environment whereby everyone has the flexibility to perform at his or her best.

3) **Facilitation of Process Architecture:** Institutionalizing a Process Architecture that will provide the organization with the means to classify its processes would help ensure the maximum benefits from BPM over an extended period of time. This architecture should provide a set of agreed activities and process directives that are used by the organization to deliver its products and services. I describe how to develop a Process Architecture in Chapter 4.

4) **Effective change management through staff:** Processes almost always have a close relationship to both people and technology. It is critical that those people who have been assigned to implement BPM are "on board" and are seen to support the project. Research has indicated that human change management can occupy anywhere from 25 percent to 35 percent of project time, cost and effort. It is therefore essential that the team responsible for implementing BPM spends proper time and effort on human change management.

5) **Establish BPM Governance:** No BPM implementation project can succeed without a proper governance model around it. Organizations that develop a BPM strategy should setup a neutral, business-oriented governance body to prioritize activities, settle escalations and establish effective monitoring. In this instance, some organizations choose to raise a Steering Group that acts as the governing body that represents either the CEO or COO.

Pitfalls to Avoid in Implementing BPM

While there are essential success factors associated with implementing BPM, there are also some major mistakes and pitfalls that can really destroy BPM from ever taking off within an organization. Throughout my time as both process analyst and business architect, I've witnessed many basic mistakes that have prevented managers from achieving the full benefits BPM has to offer. Luckily, I've managed to condense most of these into a few pages so that you can anticipate these problems well before they arise and thwart your project.

1. Not Getting Executive Endorsement

Executive endorsement is the key to successful BPM implementation. The senior executives in the organization must commitment themselves to the project, irrespective of the direction from which it originates (IT, business unit etc.). It is essential to identify an executive sponsor as soon as possible because without one your project will develop a range of problems that will increase the risk to the project. Without a precise mandate from top management, it would be very challenging for the project manager to satisfy all affected business managers and eventually the organization may simply lose interest or divert resources onto other initiatives. Executive buy-in helps to broadcast any concerns at senior levels and act as a catalyst for advocating innovation on future BPM projects.

Another way to approach executive endorsement is by establishing a Steering Group. As mentioned previously, a Steering Group should be a neutral, business-oriented governance body that should prioritize activities, settle arguments and establish effective project principles. A Steering Group should include a range of people who represent different areas of the organization (such as IT senior management, operations heads, and even client-facing managers).

As a guide, a Steering Group should generally include:

- *An executive head of the organization.* Ideally this should be the Chief Operating Officer (COO) and therefore chief sponsor for the project. Staff at this level usually have the clout to overcome political obstacles and ability to push through any resistance to organizational change.

- *The CIO or IT Director* should also be a part of the Steering Group to represent IT and ensure the right technological resources are provided to the project.

- *The appointed head of the BPM team* (usually called a center of excellence) as they will be responsible for day-to-day management of the initial BPM project and will be responsible for implementing the decisions of the Steering Group.

- *Senior function managers* who are directly affected by the project.

2. Not establishing a Business Case

Many BPM initiatives fail because they do not start with a solid business case. A business case helps to articulate the expected benefits, the effort and expenditures that will be required, and how success will be measured. The business case also helps in measuring the benefits as they're realized during project implementation. Additionally, some organizations make the mistake of focusing on buying a BPM tool first rather than clarifying the need for such an initiative from a business improvement perspective. BPM is a management layer on top of existing IT applications and infrastructure. Without proper business justification for the purpose of the project, the tool may not cater to the business needs and requirements in the first place.

3. Not Investing in Staff

A common mistake repeated by many organizations is the lack of investment they make in their human resources. BPM projects require people who have specialized skills, knowledge and experience. Process analysis is not easy and it requires people with the right habit of mind to be able to pinpoint errors and consult on cost-effective improvements. It's important that you hire people who have strong social behavioral skills and a high degree of emotional intelligence. Process analysts will always need to engage with clients within an organization and hiring the right people will offer you peace of mind when putting them in front of senior managers. Additionally, organizations can address skill gaps through adequate training and offering BPM certification to their staff.

4. Lack of Communication Channels

Communication issues are the catalyst for many BPM project failures. Lack of visibility to all stakeholders can be detrimental to a project's health and working environment. Ideally, a BPM project should have reports / dashboards / measures that can easily be digested by senior management and decision makers. These items can also include project status updates, concerns, risks, individual user/team performance metrics, etc.

5. Not Appointing Process Stewards

A growing trend seen in many mismanaged BPM initiatives is placing more focus on modeling processes than acting to improve them. This results from not appointing process stewards. These people are the chosen staff responsible for operational management and governance in relation to the processes owned by the respective Business Unit Manager. They act to ensure that the BPM operating and governance model is enforced in their respective business unit. Thus, their role is to promote BPM, act as a champion of a processes improvement culture, and ensure all process artefacts comply with global standards.

6. Poorly defined measures of success

Many BPM projects fail, as they do not have a properly established acceptance and measurement criteria. Before initiating any process improvement initiative, it is essential to measure the current performance and the expected benefits. These should serve as a baseline for measuring the post-implementation value a BPM project offers to the organization. At the end of the project, management should also expect a proper accounting of cost and benefits to determine whether to continue with additional BPM projects.

7. Not developing a roadmap

Organizations often struggle with deriving planned benefits out of their BPM strategy due to lack of a proper road map. BPM is a comprehensive discipline, and it is therefore necessary to put some thought into planning. All BPM activities should be identified in a spreadsheet with an associated timeline for implementation. Each activity should also have a list of affected stakeholders as well as estimated cost of project implementation. More importantly, it's essential that the BPM roadmap aligns with the organizational long-term strategy (sometimes called a business blueprint). This document usually defines how the organization will grow and position itself as a competitor in the marketplace. Lastly, having a BPM roadmap helps establish the ownership and governance structures required to continuously measure and improve the effectiveness of a process, over time, and how these tools can be adapted to changes in the business environment.

8. Implementing IT-led BPM

Any BPM initiative that is led by IT is doomed to failure. BPM is a business-led management discipline that involves changes to people, process, information, and the working environment. IT may help to achieve this through the use of automation engines, but IT cannot be considered as the owner of the BPM initiative. Organizations need to adopt a business-led approach to BPM, whereby staff who actually complete the work of the business are considered the process enablers and are empowered to facilitate process improvement. I will discuss why this is so important in Chapter 3.

9. Implementing Lean or Six Sigma-led BPM

In addition to letting the IT department implement BPM, some organizations may also make the mistake of delegating Lean or Six Sigma staff to implement BPM instead. People who have been trained in either Lean or Six Sigma only see the world through a "process measurement" lens and rarely have the training or skills to understand how to actually *manage* processes. Furthermore, Lean and Six Sigma are sub-functions of BPM and only participate in process improvement once a process analyst has finished developing his or her models. Lean and Six Sigma practitioners also tend to think at the tactical / operational levels of an organization and are not employed to focus on strategic-level objectives like business strategy and business architecture practitioners are.

10. Getting distracted by the wrong advice, other projects, or fads

A Management Consultant whom I used to work with once said to me that BPM was like organizing a wedding—everyone has an opinion on how you should do things. When you start implementing BPM in your organization, you will likely find that "experts" will come out of nowhere and attempt to steal your limelight. They may offer advice in good faith despite them having very little understanding of BPM in the first place. You will also probably encounter managers, who at some stage in their forty-year career, undertook process management training (like a Six Sigma course) and think they're experts by virtue of that. Even Lean and Six Sigma practitioners may also attempt to thwart your efforts as many believe that BPM starts and ends solely with process measurement—which we have learned is not the case.

If you do come across these types of problems, then my recommendation is to refer back to this book and ally yourself with your colleagues in the business strategy and business architecture teams. It is common that employees who work in these areas have management consulting backgrounds and have likely worked in organizations that have successfully implemented BPM. Also, these types of employees usually approach their work using a structured way of thinking and would almost definitely be able to grasp the BPM discipline immediately when it was presented to them. In particular, business architects usually have certification, and BPM was probably a core part of the curriculum.

You may also get distracted by other projects that arise, which will divert you from your original goal of implementing BPM. I've witnessed many instances where managers get diverted from BPM projects, because senior executives needed to react to changing market conditions—and therefore decided to place a hold on all existing projects. Such circumstances will be beyond your control. However, if you've received senior executive endorsement at the beginning of your BPM implementation project, then you'll be able to minimize the chances of the project being either delayed or cancelled.

Lastly, it's important to be aware of BPM fads and be able to distinguish the difference between those that work and those that don't. Historians of BPM will recall that during the late 1960s, TQM was viewed as a fad by many, and it was not able to gain significant traction in the United States until the early to mid-1970s. In her book *Fad Surfing in the Boardroom*, Eileen Shapiro stated that TQM was the cause of much debate among executives due to the uncertainty of its success if implemented. Senior executives are inherently risk-averse individuals, and if unsure of something, they'll avoid committing any resources or dollars to it until proven otherwise.

In 2010, a new fad emerged which was called "Social BPM." In theory, this concept advocated that businesses should have the ability to leverage on popular social network tools in order to allow both customers and staff across the enterprise to collaborate on process improvement activities. Social BPM attempted to capitalize on the popularity of Facebook, Twitter and LinkedIn by arguing that software development companies should create similar portals for organizations (either online or as stand-alone software). Since 2010, the concept of Social BPM has generated little more than a lot of discussion. This is because its objective to involve everyone across the enterprise was highly ambitious, and both customers and busy operations staff lacked motivation or time to participate in such activities. Software companies also argued that they already had collaboration functionalities embedded in their software, but these were rarely used by anyone outside BPM circles. As of writing this book, advocates of Social BPM are still unable to demonstrate any linkage between Social BPM and the non-IT aspects of the BPM discipline (such as people, process and governance). However, as tools become much more advanced and new functionalities are added, Social BPM may become a focus for discussion again in the future.

Conclusion

Over the last forty years, BPM has essentially become the umbrella term to describe all the continuous improvement approaches to process management.

TQM, Workflow Management, Lean, and Six Sigma are now viewed as specializations of the larger BPM discipline. While these approaches focus on the specific aspects of process-centered management, BPM has also been recognized as the consolidation of these concepts through the use of sophisticated automation technologies. However, the implementation at all levels of an organization by each employee is the real beauty of BPM.

Now that you've received a high-level introduction to BPM and its evolution, it's now time to get right into the details. Many people's understanding of BPM extends no further than the information provided in this chapter—and the next few chapters (specifically Chapters 3 and 4) are about to make you an instant expert. Furthermore, you're also going to be provided with detailed answers to some questions you're already likely to have developed as a result of reading this chapter. If you're confused about some of the topics that were discussed, then don't worry. Everything you need to know is about to be explained.

THE EXPERT'S CORNER

At this point, you should have a high-level understanding of the following:

- What is BPM and why it's important for organizations

- How BPM evolved over the years

- The benefits BPM offers

- Critical success factors for your BPM implementation project

- Mistakes and pitfalls to avoid in implementing your BPM project

---

Chapter 3

WHERE TO POSITION BPM
IN YOUR ORGANIZATION

What you will learn in this section:

- Understand the hierarchy of change management functions

- Where to position the BPM capability in your organization

Types of Change Management Functions

This is perhaps the most important chapter of this book. Over the years I've attended many BPM forums and workshops, and it's been amazing to see how common it is for organizations to ruin their BPM efforts as a result of not following a few fundamental rules. This is why I've devoted an entire chapter to where a BPM team should be placed within an organization. As mentioned in the previous chapter, your BPM initiative will be doomed if not situated in the right area, and with the right stakeholders. Therefore, before we get into the resources needed to develop a BPM center of excellence, it's important to discuss where to position it first.

Internationally, and within business circles, BPM is considered a change management function. What this means is that BPM is used by organizations to change existing work practices with the ultimate goal to promote business growth. BPM facilitates this by allowing managers to conduct a deep dive into their existing processes and look for opportunities for improvement. Process analysts usually have significant experience in identifying poorly performing processes as well as expertise in running projects that help managers migrate their business from their existing state to the optimized version.

However, as its title implies, BPM is all about the *management* of processes. Therefore it's important to understand that BPM must be placed in an area of the organization where its processes can be managed and governed from the top down. Likewise, BPM is a *business* discipline because it solely focuses on how the business manages its day-to-day processes.

Hierarchy of Change Management Functions

```
┌─────────────────────────────┐
│     Business Strategy        │
└─────────────────────────────┘
              ↓
┌─────────────────────────────┐
│    Business Architecture     │
└─────────────────────────────┘
              ↓
┌─────────────────────────────┐
│    Business Process          │
│      Management              │
└─────────────────────────────┘
         ↙          ↘
┌──────────────┐  ┌──────────────┐
│    Lean      │  │  Six Sigma   │
└──────────────┘  └──────────────┘
```

Figure 3.1

It's also important to note that BPM teams are not effective unless they collaborate with other teams that also have a change management focus. This is because BPM practitioners need to be familiar with the plans of an organization before they can help to change it. For example, if an organization decides to expand its services into a new geographic market, it's important that this plan is conveyed to the BPM team so they take this into consideration before making changes to business processes. However, as depicted by Figure 3.1 there are also other teams that rely on BPM as well.

The next section describes the five change management functions that are commonly used by management consulting firms and organizations around the world.

Business Strategy: This is the team that's responsible for helping the CEO determine where the organization is headed long term. People that work in these teams usually come from management consulting backgrounds and have the expertise to assess how to engage competitors, identify growth areas, and predict changes to the economy. Typically, the CEO or board will direct the business strategy team to investigate the best way the organization can carry out long-term planning. For example, the CEO may decide that the organization should buy out a competitor that holds assets that can be leveraged by the existing business. Or, the board may assess that, due to a downturn in the economy, it's important for the organization to diversify its product offering instead of focusing on one core business. The key here is that the business strategy team looks long term (usually five years out or more) and articulates their plans through blueprints or road maps that are then disseminated to the rest of the organization on behalf of the CEO.

Business Architecture: Once the business strategy team develops the long term plans of the organization, it's then up to the business architecture team to work out what the organization should look like so that it can achieve those plans. For example, if an organization decides to send its operations offshore, then it's the business architects that determine the optimum organizational structure needed for those teams to run efficiently. In this instance, the business architecture team will look at staffing numbers, IT capabilities, senior management responsibilities, governance, compliance and, of course, team roles and responsibilities.

Business Process Management: It's important that the business architecture team and the BPM team are physically located together because once the business architects have developed their plans (known in the industry as 'views'), then it's up to the process analysts to develop process models that show how the business will run day to day. The BPM team will do this by developing process models that illustrate end-to-end processes that start with the customer and end with the customer. For example, the business architect may develop a view that represents the sale of toys to customers. The process analyst will then take this view and model each step it takes to receive the order, process it, and then ship the toy to the customer. While doing this, it's also up to the process analyst to determine the most efficient and cost effective way of completing the process so that products and services are turned around in minimum time and at a low cost to the organization.

Lean and Six Sigma: In a perfect world, an organization will have all parts of its business running smoothly and efficiently. Obviously this is rarely the case—which is why organizations employ specialists that continuously improve operations regardless of changes to the economic environment, competitor behavior, or integration of new IT platforms. In the change management hierarchy, the Lean and Six Sigma practitioners need to work closely with the BPM team because they are responsible for analyzing those models developed by the process analysts.

In a manufacturing or service organization, the Lean practitioners will usually be responsible for optimizing visual management processes. Imagine you work on a floor with eighty staff members, and there are only two printers located on the other side of the floor. In order for you to print out a document, you need to walk across the room, take your document off the printer, and return to your desk. The Lean team will assess the time taken to complete that task, and, if necessary, move that printer closer to you and your colleagues to minimize the wasted time spent walking across the room. This example may seem trivial to many people who work in low tempo environments, but it's highly applicable to teams that work in call centers, processing hubs, or anywhere where speed and time is critical to the work. Therefore, the Lean team needs the process models to identify where visual obstacles occur and determine opportunities for improvement.

Likewise, the Six Sigma practitioners also need process models to measure the cost and time involved in completing a process from end to end (one that starts with the customer and ends with the customer). Six Sigma practitioners will usually take a process model and add in the time and cost associated with completing a single process in an end-to-end model. They are then able to use statistical analysis to determine cycle times as well as chokepoints that slow down a process from running at optimum efficiency.

Where your BPM team should be located

Now that I've described each of the change management functions and how they work together, it's time to discuss where the BPM team (or center of excellence) should be located. Unfortunately, many people believe that BPM should be located in an organization's IT division—and inevitably this is where the problems arise. Many organizations that have a BPM capability tend to place their teams in IT for reasons that stem back to the origin of BPM in the late 1980s and early 1990s.

In discussing the evolution of BPM in the second chapter, I talked about how BPM really came to fruition during the 1970s with the advent of TQM. What I didn't talk about was how IT companies influenced the development and adoption of BPM through the use of specialist technologies that allowed organizations to standardize and automate much of their work. Examples of BPM tools are process modelers, cloud modelers, workflow engines and simulators. All serve an essential purpose, but all require specialized knowledge to use them.

In the late 1980s, a number of IT firms collaborated to form an international consortium known as the Object Management Group (OMG). Essentially, this group became responsible for developing the international standard for process modeling that became known as Business Process Model and Notation (BPMN). The reason why it was so important to have a standard was because, up until this time, organizations were using a variety of colorful methods to develop their models. This meant software vendors had a hard time selling their wares to clients and there was no common language across the community for visually describing an end-to-end process.

Soon enough, many software vendors incorporated BPMN into their modeling tools, but they also needed to apply an underlying code called Extensible Markup Language (XML) that helped organizations integrate these BPM tools with their existing technology for automation purposes. Because of its complexity, XML was only understood by software engineers and very few other people.

To use a comparative example, Internet websites are viewed by a person through a web browser (such as Firefox or Chrome). However, when the user opens up a web page, the browser converts the webpage from HTML–the computer code the site was written in–into the pictures and text that makes visual sense to the viewer. BPM tools are exactly the same. BPM tools allow an analyst to develop models in BPMN, but the underlying code is written in XML.

How does this all relate back to the location of BPM in an organization? Well, because IT firms developed BPM tools, they naturally became responsible for evolving the BPM industry. However, when these IT firms started selling their software to clients, they sold it as though it was an IT solution and not a business solution. IT sales people also tended to use a lot of complex IT jargon which confused senior business executives. This led to an organization's IT division being responsible for BPM. Also, BPM was a relatively new concept in the early 1990s. Many senior executives didn't understand the benefits of the discipline, and BPM became largely confused with Lean and Six Sigma mainly due to their much publicized, and successful, adoption by General Electric and Motorola during the 1980s.

At the time of writing this book, there is overwhelming consensus in the international BPM community that the discipline should be a business-led initiative. This is why many organizations are now gravitating towards adopting the change management hierarchy as the means to separate the disciplines and apply them in a more structured manner. More importantly, organizations are co-locating these teams so they physically sit near each other in order to work more collaboratively.

Therefore, in terms of where a BPM team should be located, the consensus is that it should be placed in direct line to the Chief Operations Officer (COO). The figure below depicts the way an organization is typically structured—with both the CIO and COO reporting directly to the CEO.

Organization Chart

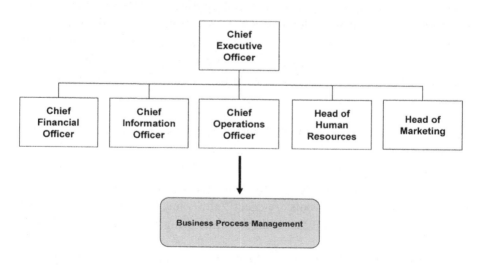

Figure 3.2

BPM should ideally sit under the COO, because he or she is usually responsible for running the core businesses of the organization. COOs are typically responsible for sales, services, manufacturing, warehousing and distribution, and most activities where the organization faces the client (for example, call centers). As a result, it's imperative that BPM sits as closely to the business as possible in order to observe, model and optimize its processes. By placing BPM in the line of the COO, the team will also have a chief sponsor as well as feel as though they're a part of running the business. Experience shows that staff from external divisions (such as IT) tends to be treated as outsiders and are afforded less priority when sent requests for work or to attend meetings.

THE EXPERT'S CORNER

At this point, you should have an understanding of the following:

- Detailed insight into the differences between the change management functions

- The importance of placing the BPM team in the organization's Operations division

---

Chapter 4

THE BPM CENTER OF EXCELLENCE

What you will learn in this section:

- Introduction to the BPM Center of Excellence
- The Four Pillars of a BPM Center of Excellence:
  - People
  - Process
  - Governance
  - Technology

Introduction to the BPM Center of Excellence

You are about to find out that this chapter is very long but is very comprehensive in detail. The reason why there is so much information here is because you'll likely find the need to develop a business case in order to convince management to implement BPM in your organization. The more you're able to prove that you know what you're doing, the more likely your business case will get approved. Nevertheless, this chapter has been divided into each of the four pillar components (people, process, governance and technology). Therefore, it shouldn't be too hard to find quickly the information you're looking for.

At a high-level view, it's important that organizations apply proper best practice frameworks when implementing a BPM capability. The reason for this is because BPM is a multi-faceted discipline that inevitably affects all areas of the organization. As a result, it's important to ensure there is a structured method used in order to achieve the intended objectives.

The quest for growth usually drives organizations to undertake a multitude of BPM initiatives that each serve a different purpose. These initiatives range from increasing operational efficiency, supporting new service offerings, implementing process automation, enhancing performance monitoring, or improving regulatory compliance. Though these initiatives are aimed to improve the competitiveness of the organization, implementing BPM may also present significant challenges in the consistency at which it is delivered, and the results that it intends to establish. If you try to implement BPM projects in isolation, without the use of best practice frameworks, then it's likely your initiative will prove costly and result in substantial delays. As a result, your organization will likely experience a diminishing return on its investment in BPM.

To avoid this, it's best to ensure the organization has a centralized approach to BPM. Governance mechanisms need to be established to ensure there is strategic alignment between process management activities and business priorities. This will help the organization to define and assign the accountabilities of each stakeholder and drive the benefits of BPM in a disciplined manner.

The approach adopted by many organizations to overcome some of these issues is to develop a BPM Center of Excellence (CoE). This BPM CoE comprises a team of specialized individuals who focus on how the processes of the organization drive bottom-line margins and results. These teams are responsible for supporting a multiple of BPM projects concurrently across the business and provide resources that are well versed in the best practices of process improvement.

A BPM CoE is the mechanism used by organizations to institutionalize BPM initiatives and perpetuate its benefits across the organization in a more coordinated approach.

The BPM CoE has three main objectives associated with it:

- **Create strategic alignment and an organizational BPM culture:** A CoE ensures that all BPM services are closely integrated with an organization's corporate strategy. This requires embedding processes as part of corporate performance and reporting systems, thereby establishing a BPM culture of thinking about business processes as essential corporate assets.

- **Converge multiple BPM initiatives running in parallel:** CoEs create a convergence of all BPM-related services within an organization that increases consistency and ultimately leads to an increased return on investment. This is done through the central ownership of standards and methodologies and the establishment of a credible authority that defines, customizes, and enforces BPM standards.

- **Disseminate BPM concepts and benefits:** The CoE needs to provide tangible and robust BPM methodologies, standards, techniques, and tools in order to ensure a well-defined execution of process re-design activities. It is the CoE's responsibility for developing common principles, language, frameworks, and methodologies for process development and process architecture management.

The CoE concept is different from a project steering group as it is a full-time team that solely addresses the needs of the organization at the operational level. It also provides a central repository for knowledge and best practices by keeping an eye on global industry trends. As per a survey conducted by the Forrester group, 49 percent of companies that experienced benefits from BPM had a CoE operating somewhere within their organization.

Framework for Establishing a BPM CoE

Figure 4.1 below defines the overall framework of a BPM CoE.

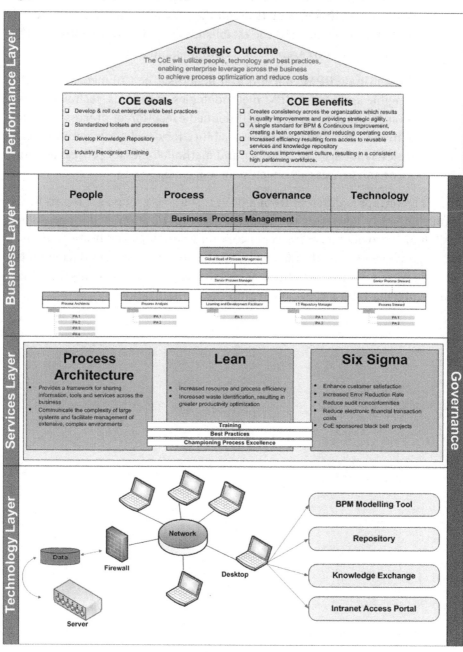

Figure 4.1

As shown above, the BPM CoE needs to be organized across multiple dimensions/layers in order to get maximum collaboration amongst the five change management teams. The four layers that define a BPM CoE structure are as follows:

- **Performance Layer:** This defines the strategic outlook of the CoE and its goals and objectives with respect to optimizing an organization's investment in BPM. The success of a BPM CoE depends heavily on how realistically its goals have been defined. With time, as the organization gets involved in multiple BPM initiatives, the CoE's goals and objectives may change. However, typical goals and objectives may include:

  - Defining the organization's BPM methodology and best practices

  - Managing the BPM process repository including BPM tools and templates

  - Ensuring consistency across active BPM projects

  - Providing guidance and performing reviews for all active projects

  - Achieving savings for the organization in terms of time and cost

- **Business Layer:** This layer defines how the actual CoE itself is run and managed. Essentially, BPM is divided into four key areas—people, process, governance, and technology. In industry terms these are known as the "four pillars of BPM" and each pillar contains guiding documentation that describes the standards the organization will use plus how BPM will be managed across the organization.

- **Service Layer:** The service layer describes the actual services that the CoE offers to the organization. It is entirely up to the organization to determine what these may be but typically, services may include training, process modeling, statistical analysis and visual management analysis. The services layer ensures that each change management team has clearly defined roles and responsibilities. For example, it's rare that a Six Sigma specialist will ever be seen trying to develop a process hierarchy. If you wish to see a complete list of services your organization may consider offering to internal clients, then I can highly recommend reading *A Framework for a BPM Center of Excellence* by Michael Rosemann (et. al). This white paper shows how you can structure a CoE's services to the framework I've provided plus place people with the right skills accordingly.

- **Technology Layer:** As the name implies, this layer represents the centralized process knowledge library (repository) and the BPM tools that can be leveraged across the enterprise. By managing a central repository, the CoE is able to house the "single source-of-truth" for all processes in the organization, and it ensures that both version control and modeling standards are adhered to. As depicted in the framework, managing this is the responsibility of the CoE team.

Of all the layers within the CoE framework, it is the Business Layer that is the most important. This is because the Business Layer defines the standards and governance mechanisms that will ensure the CoE is a success. The Business Layer of a BPM CoE is driven through the four key pillars of People, Process, Governance and Technology. These pillars are the essential components needed for the organization to implement BPM effectively.

Another result of having a four pillar platform is the team effectively becomes a center of knowledge and a key conduit between the organization and industry. The "CoE" uses industry terminology that indicates the team has reached a globally recognized standard of maturity. Reading from left to right, Figure 4.2 shows the four pillars of the CoE plus each of the elements that makes up those pillars.

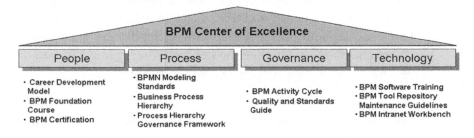

Figure 4.2

People

BPM is a technical discipline. Therefore, it's important the CoE employs the right people who have the appropriate skills and experience. People are always core to any organization, and it's the organization's human capital that helps make processes function effectively and efficiently, no matter how much they are automated. That's why "People" is the first and most important pillar in a CoE. Unfortunately, many organizations make the mistake of hiring people who lack the appropriate expertise, or they move people around internally in the hope that people will learn the discipline on the fly.

Prior to writing this book, I used to receive up to three or four phone calls a month from recruitment firms who wanted to know the industry definition of a "process analyst." They were frustrated by the fact that people included the skill on their resume—and when placed in an actual process analyst role, the organization found out they lacked both the skills and knowledge of BPM. Recruitment firms were then blamed for this error, which in turn tarnished their reputations. Unfortunately, many people believe that because they had participated at one time in a project that examined a process, it gives them the right to claim they are "process analysts." I would argue that unless a person has industry-recognized certification or has worked in an established CoE for an extended period of time, then that person should avoid including such a skill on his or her resume. Otherwise, they will inevitably be caught out.

Obviously, the first step of developing a CoE is to identify people for recruitment. These people can be dedicated team members who form the core of the CoE, or, they can be external people who are brought in to assist with certain activities (for example, management consultants). Overall, it is critical that executive management provides commitment on these resources.

The four key roles in a BPM CoE organization are:

- Process analyst (Level 1)
- Process architect (Level 2)
- Senior process practitioner (Level 3)
- Process steward

Process analyst: At the most basic level, the process analyst is the staff member of the CoE who has the responsibility for developing process models and writing procedure guides. They report directly to the manager of the CoE but also work with internal clients in undertaking process improvement activities. In terms of function, the process analyst helps manage all deliverables including those that have already been published on the organizations process repository.

The process analyst's prime role is a modeler of business processes. They critically examine processes and workflow to create process models that can be simulated, analyzed, and even executed directly by the business. The process analyst also helps business executives with decision making by modeling and simulating what-if scenarios.

The process analyst is responsible for:

- Developing business process artifacts that:
    - Provide an end-to-end view of the organization
    - Visually depict the operational blueprint of the organization
    - Facilitate process improvement and cost-saving initiatives
    - Support the automation of processes
    - Provide key insight into the performance of the business so that managerial staff can make informed decisions

- Ensuring all BPM projects adhere to the organization's process standards, guidelines, and principles

- Supporting the development of process key performance indicators

- Planning and managing assigned tasks in support of the overall CoE team

- Delivering all BPM projects on time, on budget to specification, and in accordance with the organization's policy and legislative requirements

- Developing dynamic process models that inform decision makers and add value to the organization

- Providing advice to customers on opportunities for business improvement; making recommendations and developing solutions that will advance the efficiency and effectiveness of the business

- Developing procedure guides that facilitate staff knowledge of process model activities; tailoring procedure guides for training and operational requirements

Process steward: The process stewards are usually the managers who represent the CoE but work in another area of the organization. They are responsible for governing all processes within their business unit and have the responsibility of liaising with the CoE before process analysts are utilized in their area. The process steward is responsible for operational management and governance in relation to the processes owned by their respective business unit.

The process steward is responsible for:

- Managing process governance and process improvement activities within their respective business unit

- Ensuring the CoE operating and governance model is enforced in their respective business unit

- Promoting the CoE team and acting as a champion of a processes improvement culture

- Ensuring all process artifacts comply with CoE and international BPM standards

- Developing and publishing a prioritization worksheet for the CoE team's process analysts

- Ensuring that processes that are implemented with the business units are exactly how they are depicted in a process model

- Engaging with stakeholders who wish to change any process or procedure within the business unit

- Approving the design of new and modified processes and the stopping of redundant processes

- Ensuring the CoE is assigned at least one subject matter expert in order to complete their assigned process analysis tasks

- Ensuring all processes are reviewed regularly for currency and compliance with international BPM standards

- Liaising with the necessary assurance and risk teams to perform quality audits of process models to gauge the levels of process conformance

- Collecting and validating feedback from subject matter experts and other stakeholders in relation to process improvement opportunities

The BPM Career Development Model

The Career Development Model (CDM) is a formalized framework that specifies the development, learning competencies, and promotion path for an organization's CoE team.

This model is adopted from best-practice frameworks used across the BPM industry, and has a distinct focus on IT and business architecture. This focus allows BPM staff to work collaboratively with staff from both the IT and the business architecture teams. The CDM also aims to clarify and adopt a formal policy for promotion of staff.

While employees of an organization can easily be trained to develop process models, organizations with a CoE require their staff to be multi-disciplined in order to meet the demands of its internal clients. It is not enough for a process analyst to simply model processes. Organizations require direction and key insights into their process activities. Furthermore, they need skilled staff who are able to monitor and flag potential risk areas that may not otherwise be obvious to process owners.

The four key objectives of the CDM within an organization are:

1. **Understanding the principles of BPM**

   All CoE staff are expected to have an understanding of BPM in terms of its history and background. Staff must be proficient in advising internal clients on how BPM unlocks value in their organization and be able to link historical examples of best-practice methodologies to current projects or tasks.

2. **Learning to use and apply BPM**

   Staff must have a working knowledge of process modeling. Likewise, staff must be able to use BPM software tools and make full use of the feature-rich environment they provide practitioners. This will result in the practitioner being able to analyze process models to identify process efficiency and areas for cost savings in terms of time and money.

3. **Applying BPM to client projects**

   Staff must be capable of demonstrating the success of BPM to internal clients. Normally, clients will have little understanding of BPM or its methodology. Therefore it is up to the practitioner to "sell" BPM services by highlighting its value and sharing a vision for ongoing process improvement. In doing this, staff must be able to develop full "end-to-end" process models for their clients as well as develop practical solutions that result from process engineering and process improvement activities.

4. Becoming a recognized practitioner of BPM

Long-term staff should focus on becoming recognized practitioners of BPM both within the organization and the broader BPM community. This may involve delivering key insight papers at conferences or contributing to the community through blogs and online forums. A recognized practitioner will also have an established set of core skills such as TOGAF, Lean, Six Sigma, or BPM and have demonstrated the use of these skills on multiple projects. Likewise, recognized practitioners must have participated in several BPM-related projects whereby the entire BPM operating model was executed.

In order for a staff member to progress through each level of the CDM, staff must demonstrate to management they are competent enough to fulfill their duties for the organization's internal clients.

The three levels of the CDM are:

Figure 4.3

These three levels are closely aligned with the BPM Maturity Model discussed in Chapter 5 of this book. Based on their skills and experience, staff should be able to progress through the levels and participate in the more advanced activities outlined in the maturity model. Using this framework allows the CoE team to improve its skill base and capability and conform to international standards in process design and execution. The BPM Maturity Model is a well-tested and widely used best-practice framework that, if properly implemented, will enable the CoE to become an effective and proactive resource for its organization and the broader BPM community.

Core competencies for Levels 1 and 2 are more skill-focused, whereas the emphasis for Level 3 is on skill, leadership and client-facing abilities. This is because Level 3 practitioners are required to facilitate change management workshops and attend stakeholder meetings that have impact at the enterprise level of the organization.

Level 1 – Process analyst: Level 1 staff are considered to have basic core skills that can be broadly utilized across a CoE practice. These skills generally surround the technique of process modeling and procedure writing. At this level, it is still necessary for staff to engage in client meetings but only with the supervision of Level 2 or Level 3 practitioners.

Level 1 staff assume less responsibility for quality assurance and work production than those at levels 2 and 3. However, it is expected process analysts will always press more senior staff for guidance and ensure their developmental needs are being met in order to progress to the next level.

- Core BPM Skills
  - Advanced understanding of BPMN 1.2 or 2.0
  - Process modeling
  - First tier process improvement analytics
- Related Skills
  - Facilitating workshops
  - Participation in stakeholder interviews
- BPM Software
  - Procedure document writing support
  - Ability to use the entire functionality of an industry recognized BPM tool
  - Ability to use the tool for process modeling, simulation, dashboarding, and time clocking analysis
- BPM Client Experience
  - Ability to develop models as required by clients
  - Ability to update models whenever necessary

Level 2 – Process architect: At this level, process architects are expected to refine their core BPM skills as well as progress in their understanding of business architecture frameworks (for example, TOGAF). Additionally, process architects should be able to lead client interaction and become experts in process analysis and assessment.

More critically, process architects should attempt to become expert users of BPM technology that enables them to gain insight into process risk, cost analysis and simulation.

- Core BPM Skills
    - BPMN 1.2 and 2.0 practitioner
    - Full end-to-end business process modeling
    - Process discovery
    - Process re-design (through use of Lean and Six Sigma principles)
    - Workflow management
    - Business process rule management (for example, risk, exception handling)
    - Understanding of the BPM Maturity Model
- Related Skills
    - Write procedure documents
    - Facilitate workshops
    - Interview stakeholders at the middle management level
    - Conduct project management
    - Perform surveys
    - Understand basic business architecture frameworks (for example, TOGAF, DoDAF)
    - Understand and demonstrate applicability of BPM to business architecture
- BPM Software
    - Ability to use the entire functionality of an industry recognised BPM tool
    - Ability to use the tool for process modeling, simulation, dashboarding and time clocking analysis

- BPM Client Experience

    - Design and develop end-to-end process models for clients

    - Lead BPM projects on behalf of clients

    - Conduct metric analysis using dashboarding and simulation analysis

Level 3 – Senior process practitioner: Level 3 practitioners are viewed by the organization as leaders of the CoE practice. They are familiar with both local and international best practices and are able to execute large-scale BPM projects for a variety of clients.

- Core BPM Skills

    - BPMN 1.2 and 2.0 practitioner

    - BPM modeling

    - Dashboarding

    - Process simulation

    - Full end-to-end business process modeling

    - Process discovery

    - Process re-design (through use of Lean and Six Sigma tools)

    - Workflow management

    - Business process rule management (for example, risk, exception handling)

    - Advanced understanding of the BPM Maturity Model

- Related Skills

    - Write procedure guides and quality assurance assessments

    - Run workshops

    - Manage senior stakeholders

    - Manage projects (practitioner)

    - Perform surveys

    - Align business architecture frameworks to BPM architecture

- BPM Software

    - Ability to use the entire functionality of an industry recognized BPM tool

    - Ability to use the tool for process modeling, simulation, dash-boarding and time clocking analysis

- BPM Client Experience

    - Industry-recognized practitioner

    - Proven ability to design and execute large BPM projects

CDM Skill Matrix: The following matrix provides a snapshot of the key skills required for each level of BPM staff:

Competency	Level 1	Level 2	Level 3
BPMN 1.2	x	x	x
BPMN 2.0	x	x	x
BPM Modeling	x	x	x
Process Redesign			x
End-to-end Process Modeling	x	x	x
Dashboarding			x
Workflow Management		x	x
Rule Management		x	x
BPM Maturity Model		x	x
Procedure Document Writing	x	x	x
Perform Surveys		x	x
Stakeholder Engagement	x	x	x
Project Management		x	x
Industry recognized modeling tool	x	x	x
Basic understanding of TOGAF or other business architecture frame-work		x	x

Advanced understanding of TOGAF or other business architecture framework			x
Industry recognized BPM, business architecture, Lean or Six Sigma certification	x	x	x

Table 2

The following table provides an example of how Level 1, 2 and 3 practitioners can actively track how their skills are progressing against each of the grades:

Grade 1	Grade 2	Grade 3	Grade 4	Grade 5
Cannot perform the task	Familiar with elements of the competency	Can perform with help	Can perform solo	Can task others to perform
○	◔	◑	◕	●

Table 3

Process Modeling Techniques

Business Process Modeling (incorrectly abbreviated as BPM by many people) is a methodology for visually representing a series of activities, events and actions through diagrams in a sequence from end to end. These activities range from high-level business activities and processes, to operational level technical processes that may be executed on a daily basis within an organization.

Sequence is important and essential to most aspects of business process modeling as it aims to help staff at all levels to quickly identify and pinpoint exactly where productivity and efficiency can be improved.

In the BPM discipline there are three types of artifacts that are usually created by a process analyst. They are process maps, process models, and procedure guides. Many people often confuse the difference between a map and a model, however each is distinctly different. RACI Matrices and Functional Decomposition Diagrams are also developed by process analysts, however they are not always core to their duties, and they are often developed by business architects.

Process Maps

A process map is essentially a flat file drawing that cannot be changed, altered, or manipulated once it's been developed. Process maps can be drawn on post-it notes, Power Point, Visio, Word or even free hand on a large piece of butcher's paper. Because they are static flat file drawings, maps can only depict an isolated part of a single process—which means many maps have to be drawn to create a true end-to-end view of the process. Process mapping is very time intensive and is usually reserved for the occasions when process analysts don't have access to more sophisticated tools.

Process Models

Process models are dynamic files that are almost always created in an industry-recognized BPM tool. Models allow the process analyst to create end-to-end processes including its parent and child processes. Models are also dynamic in the sense that they allow the analyst to make changes in one area of the process whereby the tool will automatically cascade those changes throughout the rest of the process. For example, if an analyst has created the task "receive invoice" which is represented fifteen times throughout an end-to-end model, the tool will automatically change that task throughout the model if the analyst decides to modify it. Furthermore, because they're developed in a tool, models can be used to execute simulation-type events that provide the analyst with first tier measurement analytics on the performance of that process.

Types of Process Models

Business Process Modeling techniques enable process analysts to understand and analyze existing processes and help identify improvement opportunities. While there is a variety of process modeling standards being used by organizations worldwide, essentially there are only two that should ever be used. These standards are the visual means to depict models that represent a process. The two standards are:

1. **Flowcharts:** Flowcharts depict the sequential flow of a process using a diagrammatic representation of activities and their connections. The use of flowcharts for documenting processes can be traced back to the 1920s when they were used for software algorithms and problem solving. Today, flowcharts are considered the most basic standard for process modeling. The simplistic notation provides a single behavioral view that can then be applied at various levels of abstraction.

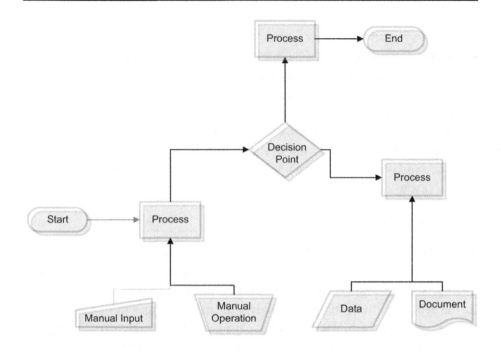

Figure 4.4

2. **BPMN:** BPMN (Business Process Model and Notation) is considered among the BPM community as the preferred standard for providing a graphical representation of processes within an organization. This standard was developed by Business Process Management Initiative (BPMI) but is now maintained by the Object Management Group. The entire specification of BPMN is very comprehensive and is way beyond the scope of this book. Most process analysts only use a small portion of the notation at any one time when developing a model. After reading this book, I highly recommend you log on to www.omg.org and download the complete specification. It's completely free and will go into more detail than the overview that's discussed below. BPMN is used by 80 percent of the world's organizations that have a BPM capability—and as of writing this book—the current version of BPMN is 2.0.

BPMN 1.2 versus 2.0

BPMN consists of symbols and objects that visually represent and describe the flow of a process. The schematic is based on the flowcharting technique (which I discussed previously) but uses more of a defined notation that provides a process analyst with more choice and flexibility for modeling a process. BPMN's objective is to provide a notation that can be easily deciphered by all business users (staff, managers and process analysts) and to ensure that its underlying computer code (XML) can be utilized for IT integration and automation purposes. Having said that, many people wrongly believe that BPMN 2.0 is a "newer" version of 1.2. While it is true the 2.0 version is an enhanced version of the older one, each is used for entirely different purposes.

If you work within a business unit of your organization (such as within operations) then you should use 1.2. But if you work on a technical team (such as within an IT division), then you should use 2.0. This is because OMG added IT elements to the 1.2 notation to make it easier to integrate with BPM workflow engines. In my view, OMG made the mistake of not clarifying that the two schematics are for different purposes. BPMN 2.0 should only be used if you're trying to process IT and system tasks. Otherwise, the model will not make sense to any reader other than a systems engineer or software developer.

The figure below shows a BPMN 1.2 model of a business process. These models can be divided into four "categories of elements," each of which is made up of one or more "element."

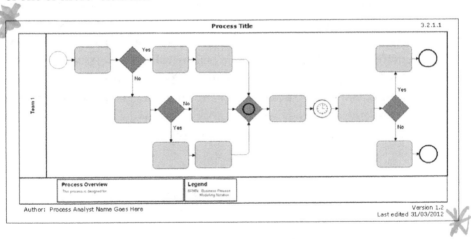

Figure 4.5

BPMN's four basic element categories are:

- **Flow objects**: Flow objects are describing elements in a BPMN model. They consist of three core sub-elements: events, activities, and gateways. An event usually represents either the start or completion of the process, whereas activities represent actual tasks that have to be completed as a part of the process. Activities are therefore always triggered by an event. Gateways, on the other hand denote either the merging or the splitting of one or more activities. Note that some people incorrectly describe gateways as "decision points." This is because BPMN contains XML computer language for automation purposes. The coding behind the gateway allows a computer to automatically direct the flow of a process, which technically does not allow the computer to stop and decide which option to take.

Event   Activity   Gateway

- **Connecting objects**: Connecting objects are used to connect multiple tasks or activities to one another. These consist of three types: sequence flows, message flows, and associations. Sequence flows present the order in which the activities in a business process are to be executed. The message flow represents the flow of information between two elements that are not within the same process pool. Associations are usually included when the author of the model needs to link information to a process (such as a document).

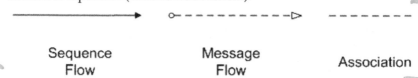

Sequence   Message
Flow   Flow   Association

- **Swim lanes**: Swim lanes are used to categorize activities based on their position within an organization. The two types are "Pool" and "Swim Lane." A pool represents the participants in a business process, and the lane is a partition within a pool and is used to further categorize the activities within the pool. For example, the activity "call client" may be the responsibility of the car sales team (swim lane) that is located in the retail sales division (pool).

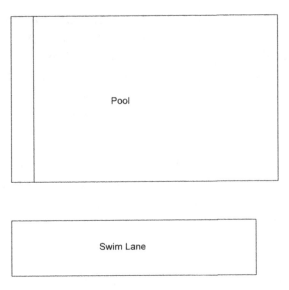

- **Artifacts:** Artifacts allow authors to add contextual information into a model. This allows the analyst to provide more information to the reader while still using a recognized notation. The three pre-defined artifacts are data object, group, and annotation. A data object shows that certain information is attributed to one or more activities (such as a credit card statement). A group presents a collection of activities that have a similar function. For example, you may have several activities in an end-to-end model that solely focus on the development of a product. An author may group these activities so it is clear to the reader that, when combined in a sequence, these activities lead to a particular result. Finally, annotations allow the author to write in additional text that may not be initially apparent from the title of the activity itself.

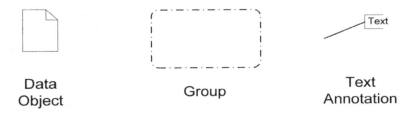

BPMN is by far and away the most common language used for developing process models. If your existing BPM capability does not use this language, then my recommendation is to adopt it immediately. In the not-to-distant future, all BPM tools will contain BPMN as their language. More importantly, this language is cross compatible between existing tools. This means that if an organization decides to upgrade its BPM software, then it won't have to worry about importing its existing artifacts into the new tool. Furthermore, it also assists with recruiting and sourcing specialists. It's far easier to recruit someone who understands a common language than to hire someone and train him or her on a new standard from scratch.

If you want to enhance your understanding of process modeling, then I can highly recommend reading *BPMN Method and Style* by Bruce Silver. The book goes into a lot of detail around best-practice modeling techniques and provides a lot more insight into the use of each of the object elements listed here.

Procedure Guides

A key artifact that organizations will often develop is an actual textual description of current processes. A procedure guide acts as a document that all employees and managers can reference to ensure there is mutual agreement and understanding of a particular process. It also serves as the baseline for training documents to prepare new workers for that process.

A procedure guide is generally written by a process analyst, but only after the process is modeled, finalized, and signed off by a business unit. It's developed after the model because a process model is always considered the source of truth, and it's the most accurate representation of the business. Analysts may also need to change the content of a procedure guide in order to write it for a specific audience. However, the best thing to remember is that most BPM tools contain a document generator whereby the process analyst can create a procedure guide directly from the model without having to write it from scratch. If your organization uses a BPM tool that does not have such a function already in place, then I recommend you buy a new tool immediately. Development of procedure guides is not considered a core function of a process analyst as they can be developed by anyone who has access to a word processor. They are difficult to update manually and a process analyst can waste a lot of time if they're responsible for overseeing a process that changes regularly. That's why it's important the process analyst focuses on process model development so they can allow the BPM tool to do most of the hard work for them.

Typically, creating this type of documentation is a reiterative process that involves individuals at various levels of responsibility. A procedure guide would contain important information such as processing steps, related documents and responsibilities, and process metrics or outputs.

The main steps in the guide process are:

1) The process analyst produces the first draft by:

   - Collecting information from process models, system documentation, reference documents, user manuals and subject matter experts

   - Analyzing information and structures within the document—for example, producing a draft table of contents

   - Writing a first draft and highlighting any gaps and questions

2) A subject matter expert will then review the document and the process analyst will make updates with the recommended changes.

   - Subject matter experts answer any questions raised by the process analyst and investigate and respond to any identified gaps

   - Subject matter experts validate the document against the process flow (if relevant) and "mark up" the document with recommended changes

3) The business unit then accepts the document and distributes it.

   - Documents are produced by publishing them to the organization's intranet portal

   - Documents are distributed to end users or are used for training purposes

RACI Matrix Tables

RACI is the abbreviation for "responsible," "accountable," "consulted," and "informed." It helps to relate process activities to stakeholder roles by identifying the people who would be responsible (they do the work for the activity), accountable (they are responsible for the success or failure of the activity), consulted (they are asked to participate in the activity), or informed (they have information concerning the activity distributed to them). Usually, a process analyst will develop a RACI matrix if it is difficult to assess the various stakeholders within a process.

Functional Decomposition Diagrams: The fourth modeling technique is to develop a process model using a list-type file. Functional decomposition diagrams are usually used by the process analyst prior to developing the process model in a BPM tool. Process analysts will often want to catalogue all end-to-end activities within a process and assess who their owners are before visually depicting them in a tool. Using functional decomposition diagrams saves a lot of time and minimizes any confusion between the stakeholder and the process analyst. These diagrams are often depicted in Microsoft Excel and contain the following fields from left to right:

- Process hierarchy number
- Process owner
- Name of process
- Purpose of process
- Date last modified
- Parent process
- Child process

Analyzing a Process Model

There are a variety of ways to actually analyze a process model, however this topic is so large that it could almost result in the publication of another book. Also, there are already hundreds of Lean and Six Sigma books that are readily available on Amazon.com which are devoted to this topic. Instead, I'm going to discuss a few key analysis techniques that are core to any process analyst's role within a CoE team.

Process Measurement

Above all else, the ability to measure a process is the most important analytical skill a process analyst must have in their toolkit–particularly as measuring processes is the key driver behind process improvement within any organization. Measuring the "as-is" process is the first step a process analyst will undertake to gather live data on the current process they are analyzing for improvement. In doing this, a data collection plan should be developed and should list the key data required and who to retrieve the data from. Required data should consist of throughput time, cycle time, queue time, activity costing, Full Time Employee (FTE) numbers, and service level agreements (SLA's) for the business process.

The process analyst will generally collaborate with the Lean and Six Sigma teams within the business to retrieve the required information. This information is crucial in designing the process model accurately in a simulation tool. As a checklist, the inputs for simulating a process are illustrated below in Table 4.

Scenario Information	Activity Data	FTE Information
Transaction Volumes and Throughput time	Cost per activity	Schedules
Simulation Constraints (SLA's)	Resources per activity	Costs
Total Cost	Cycle time of each activity	Total Resources
	Inputs and Outputs	

Table 4

Once the required information is gathered, the analyst will input the process statistics into a simulation tool. The process analyst will then focus on three core components and conduct scenario analysis in order to improve process efficiency, cost, and quality in the following areas.

1. **Staff Utilization** - The proportion of an employee's time spent contributing to the provision of products and services

2. **Activity Costing** - The identification and allocation of costs to each activity undertaken for the provision of products and services

3. **Capacity Planning** - The identification and matching of FTE capacity to customer demand for products and services

Staff Utilization

Optimizing current FTE schedules to meet customer demand can result in a reduction of average costs *and* cycle time of a process. A simulation model has the ability to indicate how the business is able to reduce cycle time per transaction against existing resource allocation. Within the scenario modeling aspect of the simulation tool, the analyst can also change the FTE schedules manually to align with peak demand using multiple scenarios and can view the output of the manipulation and compare benefits to the original process as illustrated in Figure 4.6 and 4.7.

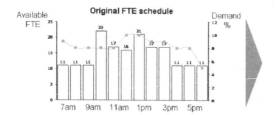

Figure 4.6

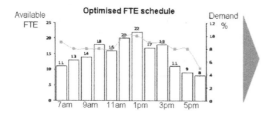

Figure 4.7

Activity Cost Analysis

Analyzing activities in the process to reduce time and cost should be the next focus for the process analyst. The primary focal point using this method should be automating manual activities, removing chokepoints, and removing redundant activities. The simulation tool can assist in identifying these points based on the simulation business rules. The process analyst will then conduct multiple scenario simulations, removing activities, adding activities, and/or editing activities that change the cycle times, throughput times, and activity costs. From here, the analyst will then determine the optimized process for the business. Figure 4.8 illustrates the activity identified as a chokepoint within the simulation tool.

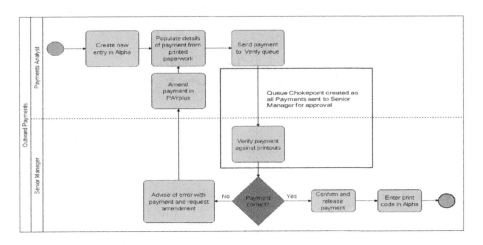

Figure 4.8

Figure 4.9 illustrates the addition of an automated gateway process made to remove the chokepoint from figure 4.8. The process simulation tool should then re-simulate the process based on the new business rule and produce statistical findings to illustrate if an actual improvement has occurred and what benefits were produced compared to the as-is process.

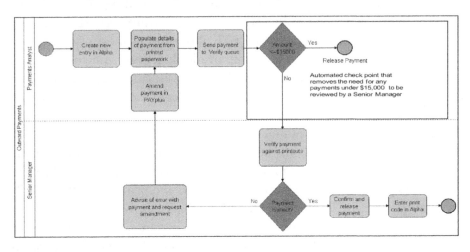

Figure 4.9

Table 5 illustrates the comparison and benefits of the process changes within the model. As you can see, the automated process change has made significant benefits by freeing up FTE utilization, reducing cost, and cycle time.

Metric	As-Is Figure 4.8	To-Be scenario Figure 4.9	Benefits
Average Utilization	83%	72%	Provided a reduction in FTE time by 11%
Average Cost	$18.04	$12.04	Average cost decreased by $6.00 per transaction
Average Cycle Time	768 hours	720 hours	Cycle time saving of 48 minutes

Table 5

Capacity Planning

Simulation enables informed decision making by providing insight into the cost and time of a process while using varying FTE numbers. SLA's become a critical component when utilizing FTE allocation as most organizations are focused on cost reduction and often overlook delivery time of the product to its customers. The appropriate level of FTE's will depend upon the type and nature of the process itself. Table 6 depicts a process that has an SLA of two days. The analysis identifies that the as-is process (currently delivering at three days) is not meeting the required SLA target of two days. This becomes a risk to the business and may result in a loss of customers or other financial ramifications. If a customer is sold a product on the basis of a two day processing time, and is delivered the product in three days, the quality therefore becomes void, and the customer will likely take their business elsewhere. To ensure quality to the customer, the recommended FTE's would become nineteen. This causes an increase in the cost per product produced, but provides quality and removes the non-conformance risk increasing customer satisfaction, which will likely result in increased business to the organization.

Metric	As-Is	Sim#1	Sim#2	Sim#3
FTE Count	17	18	19	20
Average Cycle Time (Days)	**3.0**	**2.04**	**1.7**	**1.4**
Average Cost (Per Activity)	$14.30	$14.60	$15.15	$15.60
Total Cost	$19.70	$21.80	$22.20	$23.70

Table 6

Process Catalogues

Effective BPM requires organizations to develop catalogues to distinguish business and technical processes and assign process owners. A process catalogue is a comprehensive database of processes for each business unit. It is usually housed in either a spreadsheet or BPM tool (most tools come with a built in repository feature). A BPM catalogue should include policies, guidelines, responsibilities, and service level arrangements for each process. In BPM, there are two types of process catalogues:

- Business Process Catalogue

- Technical Process Catalogue

A **Business Process Catalogue** contains details of all business processes that are used to deliver goods and services to the customer from the perspective of the business unit. A Business Process Catalogue allows business units to instantly replicate a product or service by using existing processes—as opposed to developing them from scratch.

A **Technical Process Catalogue,** on the other hand, contains details of all processes delivered from an IT perspective. This type of catalogue usually depicts the relationships between systems, data, and processes. It may also include other details such as information flows, data elements and executable code. Catalogues of this type are rarely used by process analysts and are not normally visible to standard stakeholders. Instead, these catalogues are used by IT support teams, solution architects, software engineers, and IT project delivery teams.

Maintenance of process catalogues helps resolve key issues around business planning, information sharing workflow and automation, and service delivery. As shown in the below figure, it helps to recognize the future state of the processes and identify the gaps.

Architecture Type	Future State	Impact and Level of Change Required	Gap Assessment (example)	Key Solution
Business Process Catalogue	• All staff should be able to access a complete process repository • Repository should be broken down by team and/or function • Owned by an appointed a Process Steward		• Individuals and teams use their own processes which are not formalized • Existing Process Repository is not being used and may not reflect actual processes being used • Staff are likely using sub-optimized processes	• Create an exclusive Business Process Catalogue on the organizations intranet • Lists all processes and who is responsible for them • Links to internal team portal sites • Acts as the source of truth for the business
Technical Process Catalogue	• A technical process catalogue lists the relationships between systems, data and processes • Is used for Enterprise Architecture assessments and where IT workflow engines are involved • It is usually used exclusively by IT analysts		• No Technical Process Catalogue exists within the organization	• The Business Architecture team can create a model Technical Process Catalogue which can be then populated by IT staff • Should only be developed if there is a business requirement

Figure 11

Developing a Process Hierarchy

The Business Process Hierarchy (also known as a process architecture) is a list of all process models that are tagged against a number for easy identification and placement within a process hierarchy. It is developed to categorize each process's models using a best-practice framework.

A process hierarchy allows staff to identify the processes associated with each business service as well as identify gaps in process modeling. In many organizations, process models are developed on an ad hoc basis, with no consistency in numbering or naming association. Furthermore, models are developed without a direct linkage to business services, activities or products. Sometimes, models are also developed on request of each of the business units without taking into account how each process fits into the broader process hierarchy. The result of this is usually a repository that contains mixed sets of models and data.

To overcome this problem, it is recommended the CoE team adopt the Process Classification Framework (PCF) as a means for developing a best practice hierarchy. Developed by APQC, the PCF was originally envisioned as a taxonomy of business processes and a common language through which organizations could benchmark their processes. The initial design involved more than eighty organizations with strong interest in advancing the use of benchmarking in the United States and worldwide. Since its inception in 1992, the PCF has seen several updates to its content. These updates ensure the framework is consistent with the best practices organizations apply to their business services around the world. By implementing a hierarchy using the PCF framework, the CoE can offer full process transparency across all business lines.

Figure 12 shows the hierarchy-operating model for a retail consumer product business. It depicts the number associated with each of the capability components within the organization's business lines. Each element is referred to by two numbers: a number used to locate the content within that particular framework (in the format 1.2.3.4) and a serial number used to uniquely identify the process element across the entire business service. For example, the capability "Customer Service" is uniquely identified by the number "6" in the process hierarchy.

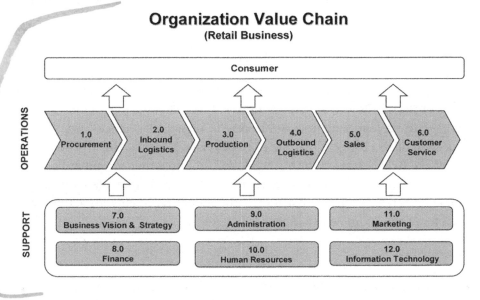

Figure 12

Each number of the hierarchy represents a particular class of process. This forms the basis of a process hierarchy whereby staff are able to visually see where a model sits within a tree-based structure. To further delineate this hierarchy, processes have been assigned to a series of classes. The following Figure provides a visual context of how this applies within a tree-like structure.

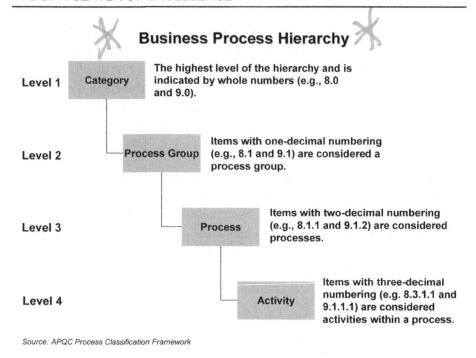

Source: APQC Process Classification Framework

Figure 13

As a general rule, the process hierarchy should not go down more than four levels of class. This is to ensure the process hierarchy is kept succinct and formalized in its representation and is easy to manage if changes occur to the process models. To see a real life example, have a look at the process model under the BPMN section in this book. You will note that a number has been assigned in the top right-hand corner. The number is four places in length (contains three decimals) that means the model represents an activity and therefore is subordinate to a higher-level process.

Governance

A lack of governance usually results from a lack of ownership and lack of process controls within and across business units—and the impact of such problems can be significantly detrimental to an organization's business strategy and operations. The failure to govern evolving business processes can result in millions of dollars in costly service redesigns, maintenance, and project delay costs. It can also result in the potential loss of revenue and increased liabilities.

BPM governance can be simply described as "the ability to direct and organize processes and clarify the responsibilities between the IT and the business side." This becomes extremely important if the organization's business environment grows more complex. Research shows that organizations with good BPM governance have better information quality, generate higher profits, and lead to more satisfied customers.

The CoE team should have clear governance policies that articulate how it manages its work, and how it supports the broader organization's business units. In order for the team to meet the demands of its internal clients and avoid the familiar pitfalls when implementing business processes that span multiple departments, a linear governance model should be adopted which helps optimize the efficiency and effectiveness of staff and management.

In doing this, it is recommended the CoE publish a set of documents that describes to clients its exact roles and responsibilities within the organization. Items that may be included are such topics as: how to submit a request for modeling services, the role of the process steward, how to obtain models through the process repository, etc. I've worked in several organizations that have a BPM capability, and most teams have published a document titled "BPM Center of Excellence Guide for Clients" (or something to that effect). Essentially, this type of guide is a reference document that helps reduce ambiguity as to the role of BPM within the organization.

The following governance model depicts the management reporting line for the CoE team. Internally to the organization, the team should report to the COO. However, some organizations will choose the team to report directly to the Head of Business Architecture. The reason for this is because BPM is viewed as a sub-function of business architecture. Many of the deliverables developed by the CoE team, such as process models, have a direct correlation to the deliverables of the Architecture team (such as process views). It is therefore in the interest of the business that a strong reporting mechanism exists for the two teams to work collaboratively. The figure below depicts an example of where the CoE team can sit in relation to the COO and the rest of the change management functions.

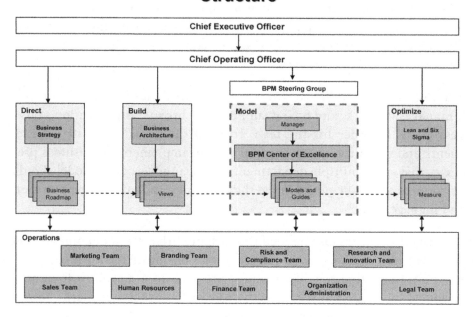

Figure 14

The second line of management reporting relates to how teams work with business units. Figure 14 depicts an organization's operations structure that has nine business units.

In order to provide a higher quality of service to each of the business units, the CoE team should be organized so that each business unit has a process steward representative. The reason for this model is so that the business units have a single conduit for all BPM-related projects, and there is also a dedicated subject matter expert where they are seen as the "process champion" of a particular area. This governance model has been established to prevent process analysts from working across multiple business lines—minimizing the opportunity of an improper balance of workload activities.

The BPM Activity Cycle

With a robust governance framework in place, the CoE will almost always have a dedicated operating model for dealing with internal clients and for developing and maintaining process models. The objective of the BPM Activity Cycle is to ensure the team:

- Understands all stakeholder requirements of processes

- Builds models that comply with stakeholder requirements (including internal and external obligations impacting on the process)

- Builds controls into processes to manage risk

- Responds in a structured and consistent method to changes which impact on processes and their controlled environment

- Responds in a structured and consistent method to process breakdowns or incidents

- Uses effective change management principles to address any process change and to communicate the effect of change

- Provides tools and guidance to assist with the ongoing management and change to processes

- Undertakes a pro-active review of its processes on a regular basis

This activity cycle has been drawn on best practice standards from global organizations that have a BPM capability. Each element of the cycle has been developed to ensure the full end-to-end spectrum of process management has been executed within an organization. This cycle has also been designed to help management run their teams as efficiently as possible in terms of managing workload and meeting the demands of customers.

Figure 15 depicts the eight activities within the BPM Activity Cycle. Each of these activities requires a number of stakeholders to be involved who directly contribute to the output of each component.

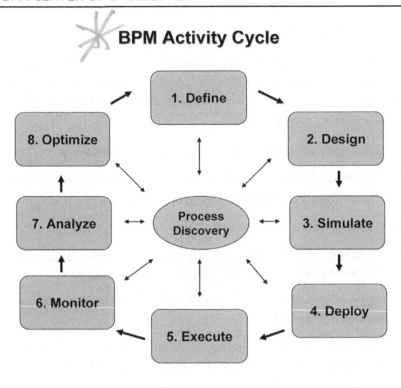

Figure 15

- **Define:** The define phase is largely dependent on the team's clients. During this phase, it is up to the client to define their requirements and describe them to the process analyst. Without a clear definition of the process it is unlikely the process analyst will be able to successfully complete all subsequent phases.

To complete this activity, the client is required to develop a work request and submit it to the process analyst that represents their respective business unit. This must be in the form of a formal work request so that all work is logged and actively tracked. Work requests are usually submitted through some form of on-line workbench. In a CoE, a process analyst is usually not allowed to receive work requests via direct e-mail, word of mouth or by any means other than formal submission through a workbench.

Upon receiving the defined work request, the manager of the CoE has the discretion to decide if the process analyst is allowed to proceed to the design phase. This step is to ensure the process analyst does not complete duplicate tasks and allows them to decide if the request is within the team's mandate.

- **Design:** Once the process analyst has received direction from the client and approval from the CoE manager, they are then ready to commence developing process models.

  During the design phase, the process analyst will develop a draft process model using the description provided by the client in the define phase. It is expected that multiple consultations will occur between the analyst and the client in order to refine the model to the exact specification required by the client. It should be noted that the only deliverable expected of the analyst is a draft version of the process model. Procedures guides that textually describe each step of the process should only be developed once the model has been tested, approved, and executed within the business.

- **Simulate:** There are a variety of methods by which an analyst can simulate a process once a model has been drafted. The first method is by using a BPM tool that simulates processes automatically and provides the analyst with a report on how optimized the process actually is. An industry-standard BPM tool should provide the user with metrics around time, cost, workload and efficiency. When done in real time, this procedure is called "dashboarding" whereby analysts can obtain insight into how well each process is performing. It should be noted that simulation and dashboarding requires the user to have an advanced knowledge of their BPM tool.

  The second method is simulating the process using real staff in a "workshop" like environment. Process analysts, at their discretion, may decide to host a workshop involving the clients that are directly impacted by the process (usually depicted in the model). This will help the analyst examine if there are any "real-life" issues with their models and allow for instant feedback from clients. Note, however, that this is perhaps the most time consuming way to simulate a process and getting all stakeholders to attend a workshop can be difficult.

  A third method involves providing the draft model to an analyst who resides outside the business line and is not a subject matter expert. Using this method means that someone can view the model with an objective mindset and without pre-conceived ideas. The reviewer should be able to follow the process and explain the logical flow back to the analyst. This is a great way for the analyst to ensure they've developed a model that can be understood by all staff within the organization and not just by BPM experts.

- **Deploy:** This phase of the Activity Cycle requires the process analyst to work with the client in deploying the new process across the business unit. However, the most appropriate way to deploy a process is to work with the business architecture analysts in developing a method for "ramp-up" and "ramp-down" activities that will cause minimal interruptions to business operations. The process analyst should also seek the guidance of the Process Stewards that reside within each business line.

  Typically, the deployment phase will require the analyst to brief all staff members who are directly impacted by that process. This will include line managers and senior staff and may also include clients external to the organization. Notification of such a change may occur via e-mail, however it is highly recommended the analyst brief all stakeholders face-to-face with support from the business architect.

  It should also be noted that the deploy phase can occur over a lengthy time frame depending on the complexity of the process model and staff involved. Sometimes it will be necessary to develop a comprehensive change management plan where funding has to be allocated to change systems and resources are re-allocated. However, should the analyst successfully complete the simulate phase of the operating model, they should have reasonable justification to convince management of the merits of implementing the new process model.

- **Execute:** The execute phase is the period where the analyst will work with the client to make the new process model "fully operational." During this phase, the analyst will identify process problems that may cause interruptions in day-to-day activities. The analyst will also make themselves available to business line staff in order to answer any questions and provide technical support where required. The execute phase should not be a lengthy exercise—particularly since all stakeholders should have been notified of the new process during the deploy phase.

An alternative to this method is to execute the new process in phases rather than operationalize all processes at once. This will allow the business line to gradually transition from the old process to the new process—and allow time for review and feedback.

- **Monitor:** The monitor phase builds on the activities the analyst completed during the execute phase. The process analyst's role is to critically examine the success of the new executed processes and make adjustments accordingly.

  Monitor activities may be comprised of formal feedback reports, on-line questionnaires, and workshops. Ultimately, the process analyst wants to ensure that business operations will run as originally intended in the process model and achieve the results that were identified during the simulation and dashboarding phase.

- **Analyze:** The analyze phase is the point where the process analyst will collate all the feedback obtained under the monitor and execute phase. In this instance, the analyst may wish to develop a more comprehensive report for management to consider—especially if the feedback has indicated that multiple changes are required. Alternatively, the process analyst may wish to use the BPM tool to conduct additional simulation and dashboarding activities that will allow them to optimize certain processes and provide a better performance for the client.

  The analyze phase is only complete once the business architect, process analyst, and client have agreed all recommendations have been documented and taken into consideration in the analyst's assessment.

- **Optimize:** The optimize phase is in two parts. The first part is for the process analyst to implement the changes that were identified during the analyze phase. The second part is for the process analyst to commence developing the procedure document that accompanies the process models.

In terms of change implementation, the process analyst will only change processes if it is deemed operationally logical to do so. On many occasions clients will provide process analysts with "wish lists" but these may not be financially viable nor provide a value-add to the business. The analyst has to be mindful of this and take into account the improvements that will be made to the "business-as-a-whole" and not just individuals or specific circumstances.

Optimization also means the process analyst has put a procedure in place whereby the end user has the means to provide feedback in "real time." This can be as simple as providing their e-mail address on the bottom of each process model, or it can be done through BPM tools where the user can click on a button that brings up a dialogue box that allows direction communication with the process analysts (similar to a messaging tool). In summary, the optimization phase should be a mechanism for facilitating continuous process improvement between themselves and the client.

At this point, you may be wondering where the Lean and Six Sigma analysts get involved. On several occasions I've mentioned that these two change management disciplines are sub-functions of BPM. But Lean and Six Sigma practitioners also need to work with process analysts in order to undertake their respective projects. These practitioners will always enter the BPM Activity Cycle in the optimize phase. Up until this time, a process analyst needs to ensure they've completed the entire BPM Activity Cycle without any interruptions. If a Lean or Six Sigma practitioner got involved at an earlier phase, the process analyst would inevitably find they would never complete their work. The reason for this is because Lean and Six Sigma analysis is time intensive. Each also tends to draw away the attention of subject matter experts who can't afford to deal with multiple analysts at once.

Setting Quality and Standards

It is very common to find that many process models are developed using a variety of different standards and notations. This may result in re-work and loss of staff utilization. Hence, it is very important to articulate the exact standards required for process artifact development.

Standards provide an agreed baseline on which process models, frameworks, methods, and classifications are developed. Standards can also help organizations to align their BPM initiatives with essential compliance requirements.

By following the checklist in the next several pages, process analysts should be able to develop fully functional artifacts that can be quickly incorporated into a workflow engine or simulation tool. There are strict rules and polices behind the discipline of BPM, and this Quality and Standards checklist helps to prevent ambiguity surrounding the development of process models and procedure guides.

Please note, the standards represented in this checklist come directly from the Object Management Group and similar internationally recognized best-practice institutions. OMG is viewed by the BPM industry as being the single global authority for process model development, and I've ensured that this has been reflected in the checklist.

Process Model Standards

Measure	Description	✓/✗
Modeling		
Has a functional decomposition matrix been developed?	A functional decomposition matrix should be developed prior to developing a process model. This will ensure models are developed in the context of an end-to-end perspective and will prevent the need for rework.	

Measure	Description	✓/✗
Formatting		
Has BPM Notation 1.2 or 2.0 been used?	All models must be in BPMN 1.2 or 2.0 to allow for metric analysis and workflow engine automation.	
Are all notation symbols the same size?	This ensures consistency in the model.	
Are all notation symbols evenly spaced?	This ensures consistency in the model.	
Does the model have a heading located in the top center of the page?	All models must have a title that describes the model.	

Measure	Description	✓/✗
Does the model have the correct hierarchy number in the top right corner of the page?	All models must be numerically classified according to the Business Process Hierarchy (Process Architecture).	
Does the model have a version number and last edited date in the bottom right footer?	All models must have version numbers to show if the model is either in draft form or has been endorsed by senior executive.	
Does the document show the name of the author in the bottom left footer?	All models must contain the name of the author to allow traceability and identify points of contact if further review is required.	

Measure	Description	✓/✗
Gateways		
Have exclusive gateways been used correctly?	Exclusive gateways should be used when only one output of the gateway is followed.	
Have inclusive gateways been used correctly?	Inclusive gateways should be used when any number of the outputs of the gateway can be followed.	
Have parallel gateways been used correctly?	Parallel gateways should be used when all outputs of the gateway are followed.	
Are gateway criteria unambiguous?	Ensure that all possibilities have been covered and that if there are percentage splits, they add up to 100 percent.	

Measure	Description	✓/✗
Tasks/Activities/Sub-Processes		
Are all activities/tasks at the same level?	This ensures consistency throughout the flow.	

Measure	Description	✓/✗
Do any of the activities need to be decomposed into a sub-process?	This ensures consistency throughout the flow.	
Are all sub-processes self-contained (i.e., there are no flows crossing the sub-process boundary)?	This conforms to BPMN best practice methodology.	
Are all activities/tasks labeled "verb-noun"?	Tasks, including sub-processes, represent work or actions performed in the process, not functions or states. Labels should not contain more than four words.	

Measure	Description	✓/✗
Events		
Do all routes through the process have a start and end event?	All routes must start and end with an event.	
Are all start and end events labeled with the description of the trigger?	All event notations must contain a description of their trigger.	

Measure	Description	✓/✗
Flows		
Do all message flows connect to a task or an event (not a gateway)?	This conforms to BPMN best-practice methodology.	

Measure	Description	✓/✗
Are elements in the same pool connected with sequence flows (not message flows)?	This conforms to BPMN best practice methodology.	
Have message flows been used between different pools (not sequence flows)?	This conforms to BPMN best practice methodology.	
If possible has the model been created so that flow lines do not overlap?	This makes the flow easier to follow when integrated with a workflow automation engine.	

Measure	Description	✓/✗
Other		
Are all elements of the diagram connected?	All notation symbols (tasks, gateways and events) must be part of the process. They cannot be "floating" in the diagram. Data objects should be connected to the activity or flow to which they relate.	
Has the end-to-end process been documented?	It is important to understand the end-to-end flow to assist with process redesign and improvement.	
Have all the business rules been defined?	All notation symbols must contain business rule definitions. These are to be embedded in the modeling tool. It is designed to capture the activities the user or system needs to complete before moving on to the next task.	
Have the main activities and gateways been identified?	If these elements are not correctly established from the beginning, the model will not be accurate.	

Measure	Description	✓/✗
Have the activities and gateways been ordered correctly?	This order is what defines the process workflow; therefore it needs to be completed correctly.	
Have all data objects worked on in a process been included?	This gives more information about what happens within the process.	
Are links included to other maps where applicable (e.g., for sub-processes or linked events)?	This allows for easy navigation along the flow of the process and also ensures that simulation and workflow engine integration can take place.	
Have the swim lanes and pools been modeled correctly?	Each pool should represent a different entity and should be labeled accordingly. If the entity needs to be broken down, lanes should be used to represent the different parts.	

Procedure Guide Standards

Measure	Description	✓/✗
Has the organizational template been used?	This ensures consistency across all guides in your organization.	
Do the steps in all process models in the guide relate to a section of the guide?	This ensures that the models are an accurate representation of the detail included in the guide.	
Does the formatting of the document conform to the organization's standard for procedure guides?	The organization's standard for procedure guides document outlines the correct formatting to be used for all text within a procedure guide.	

Measure	Description	✓/✗
Are all screenshots in the document either sized 13.5cm width or smaller (only if their actual size is smaller)?	This conforms to the organization's standard for procedure guides.	
Do all screenshots in the document have a black 1/2 point border?	This conforms to the organization's standard for procedure guides.	
Do step numbers flow in sequential order and is every step numbered for each procedure within the procedure guide?	This ensures there is no confusion when following the guide.	
Has bold text been used for all clickable or selectable screen objects or keystrokes as part of an instruction?	This conforms to the organization's standard for procedure guides.	
Bold text has **not** been used for names of windows, screen regions or in any notes?	This conforms to the organization's standard for procedure guides.	
Has italic text been used for all names of documents, reports, processes and procedures?	This conforms to the organization's standard for procedure guides.	

Measure	Description	✓/✗
Is "End of procedure." used inside the table cell to indicate the end of a procedure?	This conforms to the organization's standard for procedure guides.	
Is "End of process." used outside the table cell to indicate the end of a process?	This conforms to the organization's standard for procedure guides.	
Has a Spelling and Grammar check been completed using the dictionary on MS Word?	This ensures there are no spelling or grammar errors.	
Has the document been read to ensure spelling or grammar errors have not been missed by the spell check?	This ensures there are no spelling or grammar errors for words that would not be covered in the dictionary and also if you've used a correctly spelled word in the wrong place.	
Has a consistent tense and voice been used throughout the document?	This ensures consistency throughout the document.	
Have all cross-references and bookmarks been updated and used correctly throughout the document?	This ensures that the document flows correctly by automatically updating step numbers, page numbers, and references if required.	
Are all references within the document up to date and correct?	This ensures the document is usable.	

Measure	Description	✓/✗
Are any hyperlinks in the document correct and working?	This ensures the document is usable.	
Have any supporting documents or samples been included in the supporting Information section at the end of the document?	This ensures the document is usable.	

Technology

As I discussed in Chapter 3, many organizations make the mistake of focusing on buying a BPM tool first before trying to implement process management. This is because many people incorrectly think BPM is a technology-based discipline. As its title implies, BPM is about *managing business process*—and it's important to recognize this should be a business-led initiative and not an IT one. In BPM, the implementation of people, process, and governance should always come first. That is why the four pillars of BPM are ordered from left to right.

Having said that, adoption of a BPM tool is absolutely critical if an organization intends to manage its processes in an easier fashion. Many organizations attempt to manage their processes manually whereby everything from Excel spreadsheets to Word documents are used to list and track the attributes of a process. Fortunately, there are many tools available on the market that make this job easy. However, few people would be aware that there are different types of BPM tools which all serve a completely different function. Before you read further into this chapter, I invite you to Google "BPM software" and have a look at the results. Firstly, you will recognize that some vendors use colorful language to describe the software they're selling. Other vendors advertise their software as part of a package of tools that only work when integrated with other platforms they have offered for sale. It's for this very reason that so many organizations waste millions of dollars on choosing the wrong BPM tool. As a result of not performing due diligence, many organizations end up choosing a tool not suited for their needs. The most common mistake I've seen across the BPM industry are organizations who purchase ultra advanced BPM tools when they're at a low level of process maturity (or rank low on the BPMM maturity curve).

Dynamic versus Static BPM tools

There are only two types of tools in the discipline of BPM. One is dynamic and the other is static.

A **dynamic tool** is a dedicated software platform that is solely purchased for the purpose of BPM. It allows process analysts to create live, BPMN compliant, process models that provide the ability to make changes that can be cascaded across the entire end-to-end spectrum of a process. Dynamic tools usually come with an inbuilt simulator and repository function, although this is not always found in small scale, off-the-shelf software. However, it is very common that a dynamic tool will come preloaded with the BPMN schematic and the ability to create pre-defined processes that can be used multiple times—avoiding the need to create them from scratch.

On the flip side, a **static tool** is usually a software platform that only allows the process analyst to create flat file process maps. Examples of this include Microsoft Paint, Visio, or Word. These types of tools only produce artifacts that can be used for presentation purposes. Other than this, they have little value to a process analyst mainly due to the fact that static tools are rarely developed with the view that they'll be exclusively used for process modeling and management.

Different types of Dynamic Tools

In BPM, there are a variety of dynamic tools available on the market and unless you have a background in IT then it can be potentially very difficult to recognize the difference. The reason is because vendors will generically label their software as a BPM tool (instead of being more specific) so that they can market to a larger audience. If you approach a vendor and their software does not fit into any one of the following categories then they are not selling you a BPM tool. The different types of dynamic BPM tools are:

- **Process Modelers** – As the name implies, these are tools that are solely used to develop process models. Additional functionality may include a built-in repository, pre-defined processes, and a built-in simulator. Process Modelers will almost always have the BPMN schematic preloaded.

- **Cloud Based Modelers** – Same as a standard Process Modeler, but all information is stored in a cloud-like environment that minimizes the need to install the software on an individual desktop. As of this writing, there are still many concerns over the use of such tools—particularly in relation to data security and governance.

- **Automation and Workflow Engines** – These are tools that have been developed to be integrated into an organization's existing IT system so that core business processes can be automated. These are very expensive but are highly effective when integrated correctly. They allow an end user to log into the tool and follow a process from start to finish. For example, it allows a user to take a customer's order and follow it right up until the point a product is delivered directly into their hands.

- **Enterprise Architecture Tools** – Because BPM is a sub-discipline of Enterprise Architecture (EA), many EA tools will come pre-loaded with a process modeling capability. An organization will often choose tools like these when they have a dedicated team that solely focuses on high-level business design. However, it is common that a CoE will purchase a tool like this if they are physically co-located with the business architecture team and work on collaborative projects. Generally, these types of tools are of little use to a process analyst because they don't come with a simulation feature. They also happen to be very expensive and don't often generate a good return on investment if they're solely used for one purpose.

- **Simulators** – Although there are not many in the marketplace, simulators offer a cheap alternative to an organization wishing to assess the effectiveness of its processes. Simulators allow the process analyst to quickly model part of an end-to-end process, then run a series of events in order to measure both time and cost. This allows the analyst to identify chokepoints and other "issues" in a simulated environment. As I have already mentioned, simulation functionality is usually already embedded within many BPM tools. However, some vendors offer this software as a stand-alone and independent platform.

How to Choose a BPM tool

Due to the abundance of different software options available for process modeling, it is essential the CoE identify a tool that is capable of offering the organization (and the CoE as primary custodians) the ability to execute its core business functions against the completeness of its organization-wide mandate.

The following criterion outlines the requirements for the selection of a BPM tool for use within an organization and provides the framework that will assist in making a decision for purchase. This list is very comprehensive and will ensure that you avoid some basic errors that could prove costly long term. Some IT software companies are notoriously skilled at selling organizations the wrong tool for the wrong purpose. I once worked in an organization that acquired one of the most expensive business architecture tools on the international market. Its integrated process modeling capability only represented less than 5 percent of its total functionality. Because the organization did not perform due diligence, it ended up buying a piece of software that wasn't suited to its needs.

The core criteria for buying a BPM tool are:

- OMG BPMN 1.2 / 2.0 compliant
- Functionally efficient
- Contains a process modeling functionality
- Contains a report generating functionality
- Has an IT integration capability
- Can automatically identify risk and compliance issues
- Is cost efficient
- Contains a simulation functionality
- Contains a powerful "search" functionality
- Houses a strong [artifact] repository
- Offers BPMN process model conversion functionality
- Offers an online artifact tracking/reviewing functionality
- Offers after-sales technical support
- Contains an HTML publication function

In order to make informed decisions on BPM software requirements, a checklist has been developed to categorize and appropriately rate tools against the strict needs of the organization. The checklist represented here is the most complete method for aiding the CoE team in determining an appropriate tool that ultimately matches the needs of its organization.

Software requirements should be assessed against three ratings, based on their perceived importance to the organization in achieving its objectives:

1. **Critical** – the tool absolutely must have the specified function. The CoE team is unlikely to function without it.

2. **High** – It is essential the tool has the specified function. However, without it, the CoE team will still be able to complete their core tasks.

3. **Desirable** – It is not essential to have the specified function but having it will make BPM tasks easier to complete.

Before considering the specific requirements, bases, and overall needs of the organization, there are four main critical components of BPM software that are now standard across the BPM industry. These components are as follows:

*   Process Engine – having a robust platform for modeling and executing process-based applications, including business rules.

*   Business Analytics – enabling analysts to identify business issues, trends, and opportunities with reports and dashboards and react accordingly.

*   Content Management – providing a system for storing and securing process artefacts, electronic documents, images and other files.

*   Collaboration Tools – removing intra and interdepartmental communication barriers through discussion forums, dynamic workspaces, and message boards.

These core requirements are "standard" for an industry-leading BPM tool and therefore should always be referred to when evaluating such software.

*   **BPMN 1.2 / 2.0 compliant**: As discussed earlier, BPMN is the international best practice standard for business process modeling. BPMN provides a graphical notation for specifying business processes using a common international standard. The objective of BPMN is to support both technical users and business users by providing a notation that is intuitive to business users yet still able to represent complex process semantics.

Ultimately, the primary goal of BPMN is to provide a standard notation that is readily understandable by all business stakeholders. These business stakeholders include the business analysts who create and refine the processes, the technical developers responsible for implementing the processes, and the business managers who monitor and manage the processes. Consequently, BPMN is intended to serve as common language to bridge the communication gap that frequently occurs between business process design and implementation. Also, BPMN is the basis for process modeling worldwide, in addition to being the globally recognized method for effecting change through process management. Given that many large organizations' lines of business extend across multiple geographies, it is imperative to have an internationally-recognized standard for process modeling.

BPMN is essential for modeling the highly complex interactions between people and systems. Additionally, having processes modeled using BPMN (regardless of the tool) provides an organization with the only framework capable of running and recording real-time cost/ time benefit analysis. The software code behind the notation (XML) provides the answers as to what, where, and why processes need to be improved by identifying bottlenecks in the process flow.

Thinking beyond analysis, the true value to be gained by using BPMN to model processes is largely due to the ability of BPMN to automate processes. Being able to identify where processes can be automated is overwhelmingly beneficial for an organization's needs because it is very common to find that many key processes are repeated.

- **Functionally efficient:** "Ease of use" in software operation/development and administration is an area in which the capability of BPM vendors varies significantly. However, for a CoE team, it remains a critical component of software evaluation.

This has also been a major component of process implementation failures. Even if more scientific means of software functionality is ignored or omitted, there is still a critical need for the software to have adequate graphical representation for users. Functionality also extends to intuitiveness whereby users should be able to become quickly immersed in the software without having to resort to endless user guides or training manuals.

A BPM tool that features a working environment and user-friendly interface that is easily understandable has big advantages for the users of that software. A major benefit of this is a reduction in the learning curve of users in becoming proficient operators; the added flow-on effect of this is that user productivity is maximized within a shorter time frame.

- **Process modeling functionality:** Process modeling goes a little bit beyond putting symbols on a page and visually analyzing them. While it's the process analyst's role to develop a model and make recommendations on how to improve it, such a function should also be included in a BPM tool. For example, many tools will highlight problem areas within a model using a technique called "validation." In some tools, the software will automatically validate a model as it's being developed in real time. Others will only validate the model on request of the process analyst.

An effective BPM tool therefore needs to understand the process semantics behind the shapes and attributes in order to perform effective simulation, generate XML, and simply produce valid BPMN. This means that having a BPM tool that is capable of creating and understanding process models is critical. If the software does not understand the meaning of the process flow and the various elements that make up that flow (tasks, events, gateways), then it is merely a drawing tool and not a proper BPM tool.

As of writing this book, there are several popular BPM tools available on the market that do not have this feature. This means they are being sold as BPM tools but are little more than map generators. While this may be fine for a small business enterprise, software like this should certainly not be considered by a CoE in a large, complex organization.

For the CoE team, the process modeling functionality must also take into consideration the needs of the business architecture team. The international notation standard adopted by architecture teams is called Archimate. Although it is rare in the marketplace to find such a tool, it is worth considering if the chosen platform should be both Archimate and BPMN compliant in order to achieve true end-to-end, top-down modeling.

- **Report generating functionality:** The ability to review system and human performance is a key factor in leveraging BPM technology. Business Activity Monitoring (BAM) is the provision of real-time access to critical business performance indicators. BAM-enabled systems deliver alerts and short-period summaries of business events and metrics in something close to real time.

  Reports generated using BAM can potentially offer a business high value gains by increasing the efficiency of processes, and, in some cases, monitoring shifts of priority between conflicting goals (such as minimum cost and maximum customer engagement) in real time.

  This can also lead to increased stakeholder satisfaction by improving the continuity of the BPM services provided to the organization, as well as product and service quality, and provide the timely processing of information without comprising its integrity.

- **IT integration capability:** As the CoE team continues to expand and mature within its organization in terms of the services it can provide and the value it can offer its clients, there will always be a list of legacy systems that need to be taken into consideration as part of integrating new software with existing software. The capacity of a BPM tool capable of supporting Service Oriented Architecture (SOA) methodology becomes more important in this regard.

  A leading BPM tool should enable all stakeholders to have a firm understanding of an organization and its performance. The BPM tool should also facilitate business process change throughout the BPM life cycle. This is beneficial for the CoE team, as it will assist in the automation of activities, collaboration, (which is becoming increasingly important now more than ever), integration with other systems, and integrating partners through the value chain, etc.

  The criteria for any BPM tool should not be focused directly on its integration capability with existing systems; however the nature of BPM methodology dictates that technology has a big influence on the effectiveness of BPM tools.

  Additionally, there are also a number of other critical IT issues underpinning these key business drivers.

These include:

- Managing end-to-end and customer-facing processes

- Consolidating data and increasing visibility into and access to associated data and information

- Increasing the flexibility and functionality of current infrastructure and data

- Integrating with existing systems and leveraging existing Service Oriented Architecture

- Establishing a common language for business-IT alignment (BPMN, XML, etc.)

- **Risk and Compliance issues:** Regulatory compliance is also a factor when selecting a BPM tool. This becomes even more relevant when considering risk issues because it is paramount to the organization that it adheres to regulatory standards and legislative requirements. In addition to compliance ramifications, there are also privacy issues to consider. Due to privacy laws and other similar legislation targeted at various industries, the BPM tool that is ultimately selected would need to have capacity to manage sensitive information, while at the same time delivering the optimal performance expected of an advanced BPM tool.

- **Cost efficient:** The differences in BPM tools relating to cost are not, relatively speaking, very important from a macro standpoint. While it can be said that pricing is based on the capacity of the underlying system (as well as market demand and other economic factors), the overall idea of getting the best price is actually counter to the purpose of using the software. This is due to the fact that BPM works to promote business effectiveness and overall efficiency, while striving for innovation, flexibility, and integration with technology.

BPM is a discipline that attempts to improve processes continuously. It could therefore be described as a "process optimization" that pays for itself over a period of time. However the flip side to this argument pertains to the organization's existing investments as well as its perceived return on investment from implementing a new BPM tool.

Calculating ROI also helps you to decide if purchasing a particular BPM tool is worthwhile in the long term. In making this decision, the focus should be on looking at financial benefits such as the cost savings that can be obtained from its functionality. These savings may include new ways of implementing a business process that has potential to generate additional revenues, use process models/simulations to highlight bottlenecks in existing processes, or enable an organization to enter a new market segment.

- **Simulation functionality:** A growing number of BPM software tools are offering simulation capabilities to extend their modeling functions and enhance their analytical proficiencies. Simulation is positioned as a means to evaluate the impact of process changes and new processes in a model environment through the creation of "what-if" scenarios. Simulation provides an inexpensive way of experimenting with a real process to see how changes occur in staff roles, business activities, and overall process efficiency. Once a simulation model has been developed to represent a system or process, the BPM team may opt to find a configuration that is optimal according to performance measures and metrics that are provided by the Lean and Six Sigma teams.

Benefits of simulation are invaluable in BPM and especially within busy operational sectors of the organization. Simulation can help the BPM CoE by:

- Identifying how bottlenecks affect workflow

- Helping create a business case for deciding which improvements to focus on first (prioritization)

- Looking at constraints within a process

- Conducting a cost/benefit analysis

- Prototyping the future state process

- Testing implementation without disrupting the real environment

    After first building a baseline process model scenario, the CoE team can run simulations and identify resource costs, bottlenecks, employee productivity, cycle time, and number of transactions completed. The team can then use the results to develop different iterations of the same simulation to evaluate:

- Overall costs

- Staffing scenarios

- Production level

- Employee productivity

- Turnaround or cycle times of an activity

The team can also use the BPM tool's simulation function to try different parameters in a very short time frame and determine which provides the best results based on any set improvement targets.

- **Powerful "search" functionality:** The ability to search through existing process artifacts can be very beneficial to process analysts because automated searches reduce the amount of time it would take to trawl through all the artifacts within a static repository. Advanced search functions take this further by enabling users to set specific search criteria. This is very useful in running queries within a repository or when trying to locate a particular part of a process model.

    Another reason this is useful is because of the complexity of some of the more advanced BPM tools. Such applications have a need for ease of access to stored meta-data in order to run processes, model, and simulate processes as well as sub-processes, route, and track work. The power of any particular BPM tool's ability to run defined and accurate searches efficiently can often be a very good indicator of that tool's built-in process engine.

    Having the ability to search all process artifacts and assets within a repository is important not only for functional reasons, but also to provide traceability for users and stakeholders with a view-to-view understanding of how change can impact the business. Many older BPM tools offer search functions, albeit in a diminished and ineffective format.

    BPM tools that are able to provide reliable and fast searches of stored meta-data and process artifacts are far more likely to outperform those tools that lack this feature for these reasons.

- **Strong [artifact] repository:** A Business Process Repository is a central location for storing process artifacts. Electronic repositories range from passive containers that store process artifacts (also referred to as process objects) to sophisticated tools that serve as active participants in monitoring, executing, managing, and reporting on business processes. They come in the form of BPM tools as well as dedicated process repository systems (which are usually very expensive).

Administration of a Business Process Repository includes activities such as storing, managing, and changing process knowledge (objects, relationships, enablers, attributes, business rules, performance measures and models) for an organization. It includes creating the repository structure; defining and maintaining procedures to ensure changes are controlled, validated and approved; modeling processes to applications and data, and providing the required infrastructure to enable effective and consistent use of the models in the repository.

A capable BPM tool can manage the role of managing electronic data repositories easily. Advanced BPM tools can maintain information needed to adequately define measure, analyze, improve and control business processes.

Repositories also help to promote and support the understanding and acceptance of the cross-functional nature of many of the organization's key business processes. They facilitate collaboration across functional business units by enabling and enforcing a methodology that focuses on defining an end-to-end process.

- **BPMN process model conversion functionality:** BPMN provides a common language for constituents to communicate business processes clearly, completely and efficiently. Creating process models using BPMN is the global best practice standard in BPM. Prior to using a BPMN compliant BPM tool to create process models, other non-linear BPM software tools may have been used by your organization to generate maps.

Experience shows that if your organization has a database of maps that pre-dated the use BPMN then they're likely to be redundant and may have even been developed using a variety of tools. Suffice to say there also was probably was no "real" governance in place for mapping processes across your organization.

While it can be said that old process maps may lack continuity, key controls, and governance, that doesn't make them wrong or useless. The maps already in existence probably comprised a significant investment of time and money. Rather than casting them aside and losing all the value of this work, it would be extremely advantageous to the business if there were a way to automatically convert them into BPMN format. This would essentially turn process artifacts into process assets; that is, unified models that are able to provide real value to the organization.

While there are limited options available to convert BPMN process models into various other file types, the means of creating a backwards-compatible tool to convert older file types is not widely known or commercially available.

However, there does exist an extremely simple method of converting these file types into a useable BPMN format. Some advanced BPM tools do come with an inbuilt function that allows users to easily convert their existing process maps into BPMN-compliant process models.

This unique feature ensures that your organization's vast library of existing process maps can be leveraged for a rapid adoption of the global BPMN standard, resulting in a significant ROI and time-to-deployment advantage.

- **Online artifact tracking/reviewing functionality:** There are a great number of benefits in having a BPM tool that allows users to access process assets via an online portal. The need to have process models reviewed by peers as well as subject matter experts can be very time consuming.

   Therefore, if there existed a way in which multiple users could track, review, and make amendment annotations/comments on already modeled processes, the amount of time could theoretically be reduced *en masse*.

   The other big advantage of this idea is that where processes cross different geographies, this could potentially bridge the gap and allow for a smoother, more effective means of sharing information and opening up lines of communication between users of the system.

When analyzing Internet or portal-based functionality within a BPM tool, the CoE team may consider the need to examine SaaS (Software as a Service) technologies or cloud computing. This is still a risky proposition for an organization due to the restrictions and security that must be taken when handling sensitive information.

In reality this would have to take place within an environment that was secure, did not breach sharing policy, or misuse information policies and was controlled in a way that only allowed authorized users to view and make notes.

There are a number of BPM tools that have this capability, which run their process engine within a cloud-computing platform. There are obviously many benefits that can be provided by using this technology, but the risks must be taken into consideration when thinking of your organization's requirements for such a tool.

- **After-sales technical support:** The concept that a software vendor's responsibility to their customer ends once the purchase has been completed is very antiquated within today's competitive software market. A distinguishing factor in identifying the confidence a company has in their products is its ability to meet customer expectations and satisfaction through the offer of after-sales technical support.

  Support networks are often overlooked by consumers prior to purchase, but as the novelty wears off and questions or issues arise then users rely more and more on the availability of technical assistance. This requirement is very important when selecting a BPM tool for a variety of reasons, ranging in degrees of priority. Nearly all software vendors claim to have this support in place, however the level of support differs greatly from one vendor to the next.

  The selection of a BPM tool is a very big decision and requires a lot of thought and consideration. For this reason it is essential to have an extensive and easily contactable support structure in place from even the most obvious needs to those that are often unforeseen.

- **HTML publication functionality:** Global organizations are starting to see the conceptual role and key benefits of SaaS and cloud computing. Within a broader context, it's important for organizations in highly competitive markets to remain up to date with industry trends and weigh them against the needs of its business units. When thinking about BPM over the long term, it's fundamental for a tool to have a high level of integration with HTML, especially when using an online portal or repository.

For example, in a long term BPM project, the scale of work increases by at least an order-of-magnitude. What happens is that the number of BPM projects, the number of BPM analysts and developers, the number of users, and the number of process versions can all expand dramatically. In order to achieve economies of scale from sharing and reusing process components across a long-term BPM project, the chosen tool must make it easy to manage many more BPM projects and support many more process authors, developers, and users. Categorizing and finding reusable process assets in an online-shared library is critical. Moreover, understanding the implementation and performance of multiple versions of processes and their underlying subcomponents is also imperative.

This requirement was previously discussed when evaluating the software's online capabilities. The online functionality being referred to is the degree by which users are able to leverage the organizations intranet to access and review models that have been created and uploaded onto a secure online portal. The extension of this functionality is having a tool that is able to publish process models and relevant process data onto a web page that can be viewed by those individuals within the organization that the process relates to.

As HTML is the base code for web page design, it's logical that the organization's chosen BPM tool has the ability to understand the code, and in so doing, be able to publish models in this format and within set parameters. This function is not so much one of necessity, but rather agility; and BPM agility is crucial in the establishment of a CoE.

Some tools are able to transform models into hyper-linked web pages, preserving all drill-down levels and associations between metamodel objects. They can also incorporate a StyleSheet Builder, a utility used to define the look and feel of output without the author requiring any HTML skills.

Popular Tools Available on the Market

The reason why I'm not going to recommend a BPM tool in this book is because by the time this book is published a new and more innovative tool will likely already have been released. BPM software technology is changing so quickly that it's hard to keep up with latest developments unless you watch the market closely. Fortunately, there are groups that already do this on a full-time basis which will help aid your decision making process.

BPM experts will usually resort to seeking the advice of either the Gartner or Forrester groups. These two independent US technology think tanks publish a report once a year that summarizes the strengths and weaknesses of the latest BPM technologies. While you have to pay for the reports, the insight is very comprehensive, and they each use their own sophisticated rating system to evaluate each vendor's software.

The positive side of using these reports is that they will help clarify whether or not you're making the right decision when approaching a vendor. However, the downside is that both groups do not publish reports for each *type* of BPM tool. Unfortunately, they label all BPM tools the same which means they evaluate workflow engine platforms against vanilla process modeling tools.

Process Repository

The success of an effective CoE also depends on an organization's ability to have the correct procedure for publishing process-related information and defining those process stewards within the organization who are authorized to manage it.

A process repository is the database that is responsible for housing all process models and procedure guides for the organization. There are four key themes that form the base of any process repository. These themes are:

- **Accuracy:** Ensuring that all information that's captured within the repository is up-to-date and that whatever is presented is the "source of truth." Users must be able to extract a model and know that, when they follow its activities, they will not pose a risk to the organization.

- **Standardization:** The CoE has the responsibility to ensure all models are developed in a consistent manner. This entails the use of BPMN and standard metadata. In this context, metadata refers to information such as date, author and model number. Therefore all models must look the same with minimal cosmetic variances.

- **Continuous process improvement:** The CoE team is responsible for the continuous improvement of processes within an organization. This means that a process analyst should regularly check the existing information in the process repository and make recommendations to their client if errors or inconsistencies are found. Continuous improvement should also been embedded in the team's mandate whereby process analysts should audit all process models and procedure guides at least once a year for accuracy.

- **Customer experience:** All models and procedures guides should be developed for an end-to-end process rather than developed as parts of a process in isolation. This is to ensure the customer gets exactly the information they need from the one model rather than having to spend time trawling through multiple models. Customers should be able to locate exactly what they want within a few clicks of entering the repository rather than wasting time forming their own judgments as to which models link together.

Another purpose of the process repository is to enable a structured method of saving, storing, and accessing process assets that have been socialized and agreed upon by customers. The repository should be structured on an "organizational" basis and needs to allow users to navigate a tree of folders to access actual process documents.

A process repository should contain a hierarchy that is based along business unit lines. Figure 4.13 provides a high level view of the Process Repository hierarchy.

Figure 4.13

In this example, the first and highest level node is distinctly different from the rest of the folder structure. In a repository, the highest node should be designed similar to the Business Process Hierarchy type structure with separate folders for each of the business unit areas as illustrated in Figure 4.14 below. The CoE team should then store, save, and maintain all process model assets and supporting documents in each of the allocated folders for each business unit. As the number of models and materials increase with the CoE team's maturity, use of the folders for each of the business units may become redundant but be retained in compliance with record retention guidelines. For example, a business unit that processes customer returns for clothing may be disestablished, but it is still imperative the processes for that unit are retained for archive purposes.

Figure 4.14

The development of folders within the repository should be broken down according to a specific flow chain. The chain follows a best-practice framework and lists all process models by services rather than by business units or teams. Each number of the hierarchy represents a particular class of process. This forms the basis of a process hierarchy in a tree-based structure. The repository folder should contain at least several categories, as indicated by a whole number. For example, 1.0 is reserved for Procurement processes. See Figure 4.15.

Figure 4.15

Each repository folder should contain process group folders corresponding to each business unit and should be identified with one decimal number according to the process hierarchy. In Figure 4.15, the procurement folder contains four process group folders.

Figure 4.16

Each process group folder contains process folders and is identified with two decimal numbers in accordance with the business process hierarchy. In Figure 4.16, the Order Material folder contains four process group folders.

Each process folder contains activity folders and is identified with three decimal numbers. This is the lowest level of folder in accordance with the hierarchy. In Figure 4.17, the Purchase Order folder contains four activity folders.

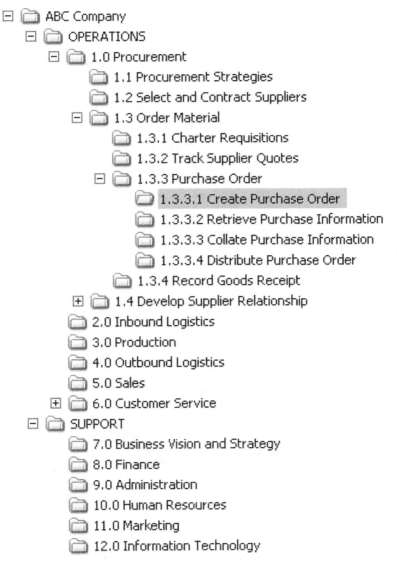

Figure 4.17

Each process model and procedure guide must be assigned a number in order to be published to the repository. The model must also fit somewhere within the tree and have a logical progression in terms of its functionality as a process within the organization. If not, then this will indicate to the CoE team that the model covers a non-business activity in which case it should not have been developed in the first place. However, the repository should continue to expand relative to the expansion of the organization. If a process model is not present in the repository, then the manager of the CoE team should be notified.

Repository Governance

The management of all BPM documentation within a process repository should be governed in a controlled environment. Effective governance will minimize the opportunities for problems in data mining and extraction. For the repository to be well managed, the inherent relationship between the content, process, and the repository must be acknowledged and tightly governed. See Figure 4.18.

Overall management of the process repository should be the responsibility of the CoE Manager. However, all content *saved* to the process repository should be the responsibility of the CoE team and the process stewards representing the business lines.

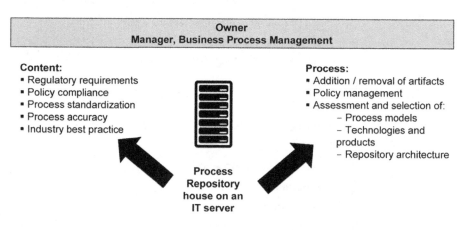

Figure 4.18

Building on this structure, roles and responsibilities should be established to ensure conventions and standards are followed throughout a model's lifecycle, as displayed in Figure 4.19 below.

Furthermore, these roles should be responsible for change requests to the content and processes they govern.

BPM Process Repository Roles and Responsibilities

Role	Model	Team	Key Responsibilities
Manager		BPM Center of Excellence	• Single individual responsible for managing and maintaining the structure of the Process Repository • Acts as the librarian to accept and review request for changes, additions, or rearrangement to the core library structure • Manage user access control
Process Analysts		BPM Center of Excellence	• Individuals who are responsible for ensuring repository structure does not change • Ensures names and conventions for both files and folders are used across the repository
Process Stewards		Business units	• Individuals who are responsible for management and oversight of a particular component of the Process Repository • Are accountable for any ongoing changes made to their models • Responsible for general content of the repository • Process Stewards should always work with the Process Analysts to initially establish the repository structure
Other stakeholders		Business units	• Anyone in the organization interested in reading or 'accessing' any of the materials published in the repository • Typically includes stakeholders who reside in the business units and reside outside of the change management teams (such as BPM, Lean etc)

Figure 4.19

THE EXPERT'S CORNER

At this point, you should have a detailed understanding of the following:

- The importance of a BPM Center of Excellence in an organization

- The Four Pillars of a BPM Center of Excellence

  - People

  - Process

  - Governance

  - Technology

Chapter 5

THE BPM MATURITY MODEL

What you will learn in this section:

- The Business Process Management Maturity Model (BPMM) – Overview and requirement

- BPMM Implementation Approach

- Applying the BPMM in your organization

- Benefits of implementing the BPMM

- What you need to succeed

Overview

Businesses today are constantly under pressure to build and sustain their competitiveness in the marketplace. Therefore, there is an increasing need to identify ways to improve the quality, optimize cost, and reduce go-to market lead time. Immature processes lead to inefficiency and delays, thus limiting a business's ability to achieve the aforementioned goals. Such processes also reduce an organization's ability to assess present and future risks. A Business Process Maturity Model (BPMM) serves as a platform for organizations to measure their BPM capabilities and achieve improvements through evaluation and comparison tools. A BPMM focuses on assessing the weaknesses and risks by fostering improvements and standardization.

The Need for a Business Process Maturity Model

A BPMM is essentially an analysis tool that an organization uses to evaluate and assess the maturity of its processes and the governance around them. These tools enable an organization to constantly benchmark and self assess the effectiveness of its processes to make sure they are managed in the most effective way possible. Maturity models provide the means to grade and measure an enterprise and assess its current position with respect to the rest of the economic environment. They also supply the organization with a method for identifying and comparing the situation as it is today against the "desired" state. Given this, an organization can identify gaps in the current state against the desired position.

A BPMM can be described as an improvement route that is evolutionary. It enables the progression from an immature and inconsistent business process to a mature and regulated one. As a process analyst, you will note that as an organization moves up the BPMM, each level becomes more specific and generates detailed recommendations that provide a stable foundation for moving to the next level. In essence, this helps the organization to identify its weakest areas using structured channels and documenting them appropriately. This in turn helps steer the improvement efforts through the suggestions of steps that are more logical and incremental at every stage of the model. The BPMM also offers a framework for evaluating the organization's IT systems and workforce development.

The following are the fundamental principles that govern a BPMM for an organization:

- Attributes of a process can be evaluated to determine its capability to contribute to organizational objectives.

- Capable processes cannot survive unless the organization is mature enough to sustain them.

- Process improvement is best approached as an organizational change program that stages the improvements to achieve successively more predictable states of organizational capability.

- Each stage or maturity level lays a required foundation on which future improvements can be built.

BPMM Implementation Approach

In the international BPM community, it is well recognized that there is only one maturity model that should be used. This is the model that was developed by the Object Management Group, and it is publicly available on their website (www.omg.org). However, a minor downside to the model is that it is very comprehensive and not easily digestible to someone who does not have a lot of BPM experience. While I recommend conducting research on the OMG version, I've taken the liberty to create my own variant that essentially achieves the same outcomes and is simpler to use. Once you read through the model presented in the next several pages, I recommend using it to assess your organization's current level. If you find that your organization sits at either Level 4 or 5, then I suggest you undertake a more thorough review using the OMG version.

The following BPMM determines the maturity level from the perspective of a five-graded scale (0-5). In this scale, 0 means "non-existent" and 5 means "innovating." It measures the maturity of people, process governance, and technology, and it helps assess where an organization sits at the current point.

Business Process Maturity Model

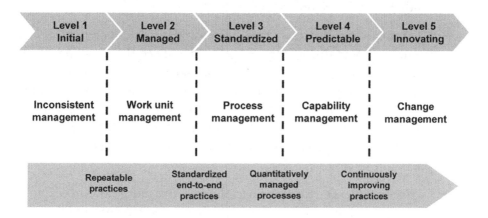

Source: OMG Business Process Maturity Model Version 1.0

Figure 24

The scales in the above model are developed based on the OMG maturity model. Each scale's description is as follows:

- **0 Non-existent:** There is a complete lack of any recognizable BPM maturity. The enterprise has not even recognized that there is an issue to be addressed.

- **1 Initial:** There is evidence the organization has recognized an issue exists and needs to be addressed. There are, however, no standardized processes in place. Instead, there are ad hoc approaches that tend to be applied on an individual or case-by-case basis. The overall approach to BPM is disorganized. Without any specific objective, the organization solely depends on the competency of the individuals and their processes for success in the absence of any proven method.

- **2 Managed:** Processes have developed to the stage where different people undertaking the same task follow similar procedures. Here, the objective is to create a foundation in the management of each work unit or project. There is some individualistic effort at improving the processes without any proper documentation; it can be likened to work unit management. There is no formal training or communication of standard procedures present, and responsibility is left to the individual. There is a high degree of reliance on the knowledge of individuals. Therefore, errors are likely.

- **3 Standardize:** Processes have been standardized, documented, and communicated through training. It is mandated that these processes should be followed; however, it is unlikely that deviations will be detected. The processes themselves are not sophisticated but simply formalize existing practices. The objective here is to make use of infrastructure in organizational processes and the related process assets. The goal is consistency through automation and delivery of the products and services.

- **4 Predictable:** During this stage, the objective moves towards exploiting the capability of the organization's process structure and its associated process assets to realize predictable results. The BPM team monitors and measures compliance with procedures and takes action where processes appear not to be working effectively. Predictable and constantly improving, these processes provide good practice. BPM automation and modeling tools are used in a limited or fragmented way. This stage in the maturity model can be described as "capability management."

- **5 Innovating:** The final stage is the most structured and competent. The objective at this level is to manage processes without turning out defective products or services. At this level, processes have been optimally refined from the results of continuous improvement and maturity modeling with other enterprises. IT is used in an integrated way to automate the workflow, providing tools to improve quality and effectiveness, and making the enterprise quick to adapt.

Applying BPMM in your organization

Let's try to apply the BPMM model described above to any organization. Again, any maturity model should always focus on the "four pillars" of BPM. In case you've forgotten them, they are:

- People
- Process
- Governance
- Technology

People: If we look at the people dimension of BPM, we will see how implementing such a measurement system will quickly identify weaknesses in training, skill, and experience. From the table below, we can see how process culture strengthens when individual performance measures and processes are interrelated.

Let us look at an example for the purpose of understanding how BPMM can positively impact a business by adopting a standardization of work practices. It can be seen in the table below that an organization's process culture will strengthen if individual performance measures are formally tied to processes.

Defi-nition	Level 0 Does not exist	Level 1 Initial	Level 2 Managed	Level 3 Standard-ized	Level 4 Predictable	Level 5 Innovating
Func-tional Train-ing	No staff train-ing or aware-ness of BPM	Under-standing of BPM taught by the indi-vidual	Some designated staff have completed some form of BPM training	All desig-nated staff have com-pleted for-mal BPM training	Some staff are indus-try- accred-ited process architects	Many staff are industry-accredited business architects
Per-for-mance mea-sures	No perfor-mances mea-sures exist	Adherence to BPM method-ology is informally recognized	Process manage-ment is embedded in staff job descrip-tions	Team lead-ers have assigned KRAs to staff around process manage-ment	Individual perfor-mance measures have been directed at the divi-sional level	Individual performance measures have been directed at the enterprise level
Soft-ware train-ing	Staff have never been exposed to a BPM tool	Staff do not use a BPM tool although one may exist	Some designated staff are trained to use a BPM tool	All desig-nated staff have been given for-mal BPM tool train-ing	All staff use a BPM tool to model processes	Staff are able to conduct simulation and execut-able activities using a BPM tool
Lead-ership	No leader-ship exists	Individu-als lead process manage-ment	Individual teams lead process manage-ment	Process manage-ment is led and endorsed by execu-tive	Executive is accountable for process manage-ment	Process man-agement is institutional-ized across the enterprise

	Staff do not have access to a process repository	Under-standing of reposi-tory man-agement is self-taught	Some staff have been trained how to manage the reposi-tory	All staff have been trained on how to manage the repository		
Repos-itory train-ing	Staff do not have access to a process repository	Under-standing of reposi-tory man-agement is self-taught	Some staff have been trained how to manage the reposi-tory	All staff have been trained on how to manage the repository	N/A	N/A

Table 9

Process: Standardization ensures consistency and repeatability when developing and executing processes in a BPM tool. Management must take care to develop viable solutions that will document and standardize processes as well as create the right working environment and employ the right people to handle those processes. Let us examine what typically occurs when an organization fails to adopt process standardization against the following five categories:

- **Documentation of Process:** Organizations in the initial stage do not have any documentation or have few documented processes.

- **Stewardship of Process:** No ownership of processes is identified in most organizations prior to implementation of BBMM.

- **Improvement Methodology for Processes:** Initially there is no methodology involved in the improvement of processes (such as Lean or Six Sigma).

- **Standardization of Processes:** No processes are the same and all appear to perform a distinctly different function.

- **Standards / Taxonomy of Processes:** Initially no standards for processes model development exist other than the BPMN notation itself.

The following table shows what happens when an organization begins to use the BPMM. The table also shows how easy it is to make improvements by making just a few practical changes to how processes are modeled, owned, and categorized.

Definition	Level 0 Does not exist	Level 1 Initial	Level 2 Managed	Level 3 Standard-ized	Level 4 Predict-able	Level 5 Innovat-ing
Process documen-tation	Zero to few processes have been docu-mented	Ad hoc, down to the indi-vidual	Some docu-mented using different stan-dards, but not nec-essarily updated	All docu-mented in a BPM tool using BPMN	Process documen-tation is stored in a central repository	All pro-cess doc-umen-tation incorpo-rates the full end-to-end design of a process
Process steward-ship	None identified	None iden-tified	Some leaders have taken on informal owner-ship	Process stewards are identi-fied with clearly defined roles and responsi-bilities	Process stewards actively manage the pro-cess	Single global process steward actively manag-ing the process
Process improve-ment methodol-ogy	No meth-odology exists	Method-ology is applied by the indi-vidual	Method-ology is randomly applied by the team	Team is directed to apply meth-odology by senior manage-ment	Meth-odology has been applied and ben-efits real-ized	Team has a culture of con-tinuous improve-ment
Process standard-ization	No pro-cesses are standard-ized	Some processes have been identified as similar	All pro-cesses have been reviewed for stan-dardiza-tion	Some pro-cesses have been stan-dardized	All pro-cesses are standard-ized	Processes have been standard-ized and optimized using Lean and Six Sigma

Process standards and taxonomy	No standards exist	Some models have a standard but are not in BPMN	Some models are in BPMN	All models are in BPMN	Models are layered in BPMN	Models are layered and linked in BPMN

Table 10

Governance: Some BPM experts argue that "governance" should be the first component of the BPMM that should be implemented. Either way, making improvements to BPM governance calls for senior management to help facilitate the organization's transition through each of the BPMM levels. The table below provides a clear method for helping an organization make systematic changes to its governance structure so that BPM implementation can be realized.

	Level 0 Does not exist	Level 1 Initial	Level 2 Managed	Level 3 Standardized	Level 4 Predictable	Level 5 Innovating
Definition						
Strategy and alignment	No goals or objectives exist	Managed by individual teams	Informally directed by the executive	Directed by the executive, published and transparent to all staff	N/A	N/A
Change control	No change management process exists	Team leads review; changes on an ad hoc basis	A formal change management process exists within the team	A centralized change management register exists	Change control is reviewed on a periodic basis by the division	Change control is reviewed on a periodic basis by the organization

Risk	No assessment is undertaken	Ad hoc, down to the individual	Risk assessment approach is documented, but not governed	Risk assessment is governed and risk mitigation strategies are deployed	A risk assessment for all processes is conducted on a yearly basis	N/A
Process architecture	No process management methodology exists	Artifacts are developed ad hoc	Artifacts are developed according to team	Artifacts are developed according to service or product but by business line only	Artifacts are developed end-to-end (start and end with the customer)	Artifacts are modeled according to the process hierarchy value chain
Quality	No review is undertaken	Individuals review quality depending on use of process artifact	Team member selectively reviews artifacts for quality	An informal quality and accuracy check exists	Process models do not get published unless checked off against the organizational quality and standards guide	Process models are audited annually for quality and accuracy

Table 11

Technology: In the context of the BPMM, technology only refers to developing a process repository and the acquisition of an industry recognized BPM tool. The OMG BPMM will provide you with more detail on how to apply technological improvements to your BPM capability, but I would argue that both the repository and the BPM tool are the only two platforms an organization needs until it has reached Levels 3 or 4. It is also important to note that implementation of these platforms should be left until the end—particularly given that the people, process, and governance pillars are more critical to the organization than the adoption of BPM technology.

Defini-tion	Level 0 Does not exist	Level 1 Initial	Level 2 Managed	Level 3 Standardized	Level 4 Predictable	Level 5 Innovating
Reposi-tory usage	Artifacts are stored on indi-vidual drives	Arti-facts are stored on team drives	Artifacts are stored on a team site, but can only be viewed by the team	Artifacts are stored on an intranet site, but are only available to the business unit	Process documen-tation is stored on a process repository, but with no classifica-tion	Artifacts are stored on a process repository and are categorized according to the process hierarchy
Tool usage	No tool identified	The BPM tool is used on an ad hoc basis	Team uses the BPM tool for devel-oping all process artifacts	The division uses the BPM tool for devel-oping all pro-cess artifacts	N/A	N/A

Table 12

Other Considerations when Implementing the BPMM

The success of the maturity model is dependent on management's ability to ignore the constant changes that face an organization. There will always be new IT systems introduced, and processes will always need to be amended. However, achieving a Level 5 rating will never occur if management becomes continuously distracted by constant challenges to the organization. Here are some issues management needs to consider when improving the organization's BPM capability:

1. While engaging in BPM-related projects, managers should always aim to use proven standardized methods of building such a capability; other-wise, they'll put the project in jeopardy. This is particularly common when managers attempt to create their own maturity models of frameworks.

2. Managers need to ensure that when a process is modeled by a process ana-lyst, it actually represents what occurs in real time in the business unit.

Often, the process followed by a business unit is completely different than how it's represented in a process model. When this occurs, it means there is a lack of governance in the organization; process analysts and business units are not communicating with each other. An organization has the ability to make significant improvements to its BPM capability here. Appointing process stewards and putting a governance mechanism in place is a simple task.

3. The BPMM ensures that complete process transparency occurs across the organization. Sometimes managers are caught off guard when a change to a process occurs in one area of the organization, and they're not aware of that change. Furthermore, some managers will attempt to develop a new process from scratch when it's already being used in another business unit. This issue is particularly common for larger organizations that have around 5,000 or more employees. By creating standardized processes, an organization can simplify the steps required to complete a business activity and thus streamline an end-to-end process.

4. Another critical aspect of the BPMM is that, *when followed*, it makes it far easier to work with vendors, consultants, and suppliers. When outsourcing IT or other business services, an organization should have the ability to develop a proposal that requests a standard set of services and products that, in turn, makes it easier to be delivered by a vendor. In reverse, an organization with a mature BPM capability also has the ability to assess the suitability of vendors prior to outsourcing any work.

5. Implementation of the BPMM also solves the serious need for how an organization develops the foundations of a business. You will recall that I talked about this in the introduction to this book. Many organizations have poorly structured management systems in place which leads to all sorts of problems. It is essential in any business to cut operational costs and to strengthen organizational agility. There are many examples of enterprises wasting millions of dollars by attempting to fix their businesses, particularly through IT. The BPMM can play a vital role by developing a strong business foundation and standard practice in process management. It also helps if the right people are involved and provided with proper training, so that the organization is better positioned to achieve its growth objectives.

THE EXPERT'S CORNER

At this point, you should have a high-level understanding of the following:

- Why organizations need BPMM

- Fundamental principles governing BPMM

- BPMM implementation approach

- Applying BPMM in your organization

- Other considerations when implementing the BPMM

Chapter 6

QUESTIONS MANAGEMENT WILL ASK YOU

What you will learn in this section:

Frequently asked questions on BPM on areas covering;

- General

- People

- Process

- Governance

- Technology

Now that you've learned about what makes a BPM Center of Excellence, it is time to start putting plans in place to actually develop one for your organization. If you already have a CoE, then I hope the framework I've discussed has provided you with options on how things can be done better.

In Chapter 2, I talked about some of the pitfalls you're likely to experience when trying to implement BPM. From my experience, the most common difficulty is actually being able to convince others of the merits of introducing such a discipline. It's very common to find that both staff and managers have never heard of BPM, let alone any of its frameworks or methodologies. Certainly, many will of heard of Lean and Six Sigma, but that's only because they've been publicized a lot more than BPM.

As you develop your plans for BPM implementation, it's likely you'll need to hold workshops and meetings with stakeholders to discuss their involvement. I can guarantee you that you will initially find resistance, particularly due to that fact that human nature resists any form of change. As a result, I've written a series of the most common questions you're likely to receive by both staff and managers. It's a good idea to memorize the answers in the context of your organization, so that no matter how tough the question, you will always be able to answer your peers with authority and conviction. Furthermore, the answers to frequently asked questions should also help clarify your understanding of some specific BPM topics that were discussed in the earlier chapters.

General

What is BPM?

Business Process Management (BPM) is the discipline of promoting business effectiveness and efficiency through the use of a globally recognized methodology. BPM deals with identifying all the processes associated with the organization, analyzing them for efficiency and effectiveness, measuring the results over a period of time, and optimizing these processes.

What kind of services does a BPM team provide?

There are two core service offerings a BPM team provides its clients. The first is process modeling, and the second is procedure writing. Within the process modeling component, the team is expected to conduct a full analysis of process efficiency and effectiveness by using methodologies such as dashboarding and simulation. Process analysts will also identify new processes and optimize existing ones using a globally recognized methodology. Once processes have been optimized and modeled, the process analyst is then responsible for writing the procedure guides.

What is the difference between BPM, Enterprise Architecture, and Business Architecture?

BPM is the practice of managing and modeling granular processes at the operational level of a business. Enterprise architecture is the practice of aligning a corporate strategy with high-level business models and IT. Enterprise architects work at the "strategic" level of an organization and need BPM analysts to design process models at the worker/operational level. The term business architecture is used to describe the sub-discipline whereby the architect solely focuses on business design.

Why is a BPM Center of Excellence important for an organization?

By having a dedicated BPM team, managers can draw on the expertise the BPM team provides without having to rely on their own staff for process analysis and procedure writing. The BPM team operates as a "center of excellence," which means its role is to maintain an awareness of international best practices and up-to-date BPM methodologies.

What is a BPM Maturity Model?

The BPM Maturity Model, sometimes known as the BPM Maturity Curve, refers to a methodology for developing a BPM capability within an organization. It allows the organization to assess how well its BPM team can meet the demands of its clients and describes what improvements an organization needs to make in order to have a fully functional, effective team. The model assesses the maturity of the "four pillars" of BPM—people, process, governance, and technology.

From a BPM perspective, what are some of the common issues any business faces?

The most common issues across business lines are: lack of process standardization, no process re-use, poorly described procedure guides, complicated process maps, and use of redundant process maps. All these issues can be identified by the organization's BPM team and can be addressed under an internal reform project.

I already have many business analysts on my team, what additional value can BPM provide my business?

Business analysts and process analysts perform two completely separate functions. When working collaboratively, both can produce results that improve operational performance. A business analyst is a generic term used to describe a staff member with research and analysis skills that allow them to gather data, develop reports, and assist with the execution of a project. A process analyst describes someone who has certification in identifying and measuring the performance of business processes and experience in helping organizations transform their operations to achieve an optimal state. Through the use of specialist software tools, a process analyst can interpret that vision through process models and simulation techniques.

Is BPM able to advise on best practices in other industries?

BPM is a universal practice that can be ported across to any industry. The original need for BPM derived from the manufacturing industry during the 1970's and was later modified to be applicable to service industries such as the banking and retail sectors. Therefore, the BPM methodology can (almost) be used for any organization, regardless of business strategy or objectives.

People

Why is BPM important for my staff?

There are several reasons why BPM is important for your staff, and they are as follows:

- Decreases employee workloads for undesirable work

- Eliminates non-value added activities

- Improves employee morale/team spirit

- Improves internal communication between departments and groups

- Improves use of workspace

- Increases employee and process productivity

- Reduces cycle time of production/process

- Reduces process steps

- Simplifies processes and workflow steps

Who are BPM's key stakeholders?

BPM's key stakeholders are team managers and team members of an organization who work within all areas of the business. Ultimately, BPM is an enterprise-level discipline that affects all areas of the organization.

Who can I approach in the BPM team if I would like some work done in my business?

All business units should have an allocated process steward that represents the BPM team. More technical inquiries can be resolved by the manager of the BPM team.

Instead of modeling our activities, why not invest more in our subject matter experts to enhance our on-the-job training capabilities?

On the job training capabilities are an important and required service; however, investing in training without documenting and modeling activities can result in transfer of incorrect habits and "perceived" knowledge. By clearly referring to a process, team members with various levels of experience can leverage a detailed and agreed document as a source of truth.

To what extent is BPM concerned with the "socializing" (i.e., People) aspect when implementing change?

As a part of the BPM operating model, it is imperative that internal clients are kept in the loop with the progress of BPM projects. Process analysts will work collaboratively with clients to ensure all processes are properly captured and documented within the process models and procedure guides. The "socialization" aspect plays an important role prior to the "deployment" phase. The analyst will need management approval before new or modified processes are introduced within a business line.

Is it true that streamlining processes usually results in jobs being lost?

No. Streamlining processes will not result in jobs being lost. Rather, streamlining processes will have the following benefits:

- Improves the ability to serve external customers with greater consistency

- Creates new customer opportunities

- Builds company reputation

- Improves market position relative to competitors

- Enables service level agreement (SLA) obligations

These benefits will create an environment of continuous improvement and promote growth within the business units.

Process

Can you describe the BPM Process Hierarchy?

A BPM Process Hierarchy (sometimes known as a Process Architecture) is the highest group of processes that are performed by an organization. When these processes (known as categories) are placed in a sequential order, they form a value chain. Take the example of a business that sells cars. An example value chain would be:

1. Sales

2. Fulfillment

3. Servicing

4. Product Marketing and Development

5. Operations

Under each of these categories are sub-processes that describe exactly how the business manages itself on a day-to-day basis. Take the "servicing" activity as an example. This activity would likely list all the processes that allow a customer to hand over their car for service and maintenance. Such processes may include: the customer dropping their car off at the service center, the tasks the technicians undertake to conduct the maintenance, and the customer collecting their car once the maintenance has been completed.

All processes found within these categories should replace the processes that are attributed to siloed lines of business. The concept behind this is that an organization moves away from a business-line centric process (siloed in their design) and progresses toward processes that make up an end-to-end value chain. Once developed and agreed upon by the organization, the Business Process Hierarchy should be housed in a Process Repository.

What are some of the methodologies used in BPM?

There are several methodologies used in BPM that manage people, process, governance, and technology. From a day-to-day perspective, a BPM team will use the BPM operating model to handle requests for work. From a modeling perspective, a team uses BPMN, which is an internationally used modeling language. There are also methodologies relating to metric analysis, dashboarding, and simulation. Examples include time clocking, 3D event simulation, and "choke point" analysis.

What is "preventive management"?

Preventive management is a term that refers to risk identification. It is the responsibility of the process steward and business subject matter expert to identify risk in a process. However, this function should also be expected of a process analyst as part of their core duties.

How will I know whether my processes are optimized?

Business processes can only be improved to a point. But they must still be monitored to ensure they are meeting a particular level of performance. Optimization is a part of the "continuous improvement" process and is an activity that never ends. However, to find out if a process has improved, a process analyst will take a measurement of a process at the beginning of their analysis and compare it to the optimized version once they've had the chance to consult with internal clients.

Why does an organization need to document every single activity in process models and procedure documents?

Capturing every process within an end-to-end value chain is essential. Managers and their staff must be able to have an absolute understanding of their business before they can measure it and subsequently optimize it. By not capturing all activities, the organization can lose essential resources such as unnecessary labor costs. By documenting all processes, the organization can minimize its risk and ensure that it meets strict legal requirements.

What is "business process interoperability?"

Process interoperability refers to processes that can work seamlessly with other processes. Each process has a description and definition of what task it is expected to perform. Interoperability therefore means the process analyst should only use previously defined and standardized processes to build that process model.

Governance

What do you mean by "driving a process view across the organization"?

The Business Process Hierarchy is a visual representation of all core processes that reside within an organization. The hierarchy is the best means for developing a complete end-to-end view of the organization and all the functions it performs as a business enterprise. This approach is the preferred method used by process analysts as it prevents an organization from randomly developing process models in isolation without any relation to each other.

Are there any globally recognized quality standards for BPM?

Yes. All BPM standards are developed and mandated by the Object Management Group (www.omg.org). This organization is supported by the international BPM community and has subsequently become the recognized authority for BPM development. In terms of standards, BPMN is used for modeling and the BPM Maturity Model for capability development. For development of the Business Process Hierarchy, APQC (www.apqc.org) is seen as the international standard among practitioners. All these standards are globally recognized and are considered "best-practice."

Can BPM help find opportunities to structure my business better?

Yes. It is the role of the process analyst to critically examine each activity within an end-to-end process and examine opportunities for improvement. Through this approach, a process analyst will usually work with an architect from the business architecture team to develop optimal business models.

How can BPM help me reduce my costs?

BPM is an essential method used to optimize business operations. Process analysts look for duplicate processes or unnecessary processes within an end-to-end model. By removing these activities, a business line is able to save on operating costs. This can be quantified in both time and money.

Technology

What are some of the more common tools used in BPM?

In the BPM discipline there are two categories of BPM tools. They are:

- Static tools
- Dynamic tools

Microsoft Visio is an example of a static tool that only allows analysts to develop pictures of processes.

Process Modeling tools and Automation Workflow Engines are examples of dynamic tools that allow an analyst to conduct dashboarding and develop "interactive" models so that customers and analysts can work collaboratively on projects. Dynamic tools allow for process re-use, use a special library, and can automatically conduct assessments of the efficiency of a model.

Simulators allow analysts to develop 3D models of process and execute real-time simulated activities that can pinpoint choke points in processes and provide a visualization of an activity.

Can BPM assist me in automating some of my activities?

Yes. This is a core function of any BPM team. Once the Process Hierarchy has been fully developed, internal clients should be able to "choose" which processes require automation so that it can be completed without a human in the loop.

How can BPM assist my business with implementation of a new IT system?

The BPM team, in conjunction with the business architecture team, can provide "to-be" models of what a process will look like once an IT system has been implemented.

I am thinking of purchasing a new IT system, can the BPM team assist with drafting my user requirements?

Business architecture teams are responsible for assessing capabilities such as IT and ensuring they meet the business requirements of an organization.

How can BPM ensure that new IT systems are aligned with organizational strategy?

This is the core role of a business architecture team and not a function of the BPM Center of Excellence.

THE EXPERT'S CORNER

At this point, you should have a high-level understanding of the following:

- How to handle the tough questions that management will throw at you.

Chapter 7

THE EXPERT'S DICTIONARY

What you will learn in this section:

- All common terminology associated with BPM

I've put the following dictionary together to provide you with a list of common terms associated with BPM. While there are literally thousands of words relating to BPM, I've only included the ones that are important to process analysts and business managers. The terms listed here are also referenced in the chapters of this book, which should help you just in case you get stuck.

A

Activity

Also known as a "task," an activity is a single-step process that requires completion in order for a process to continue. Sending a form to a customer is an activity. Likewise, an activity is receiving a phone call from a supplier. In BPMN, activities are represented with a rectangle.

Activity Analysis Worksheet

See *Functional Decomposition Diagram.*

Activity Cost Worksheet

A Functional Decomposition Diagram that has been solely developed to list costs associated with the execution of each process. The Lean and Six Sigma analysts usually develop these during the "optimize" phase of the BPM Activity Cycle.

Activity-Based Costing

A method used to assess the cost for each activity in a sequential process with the objective of removing activities that do not add value to the organization or the customer. Lean and Six Sigma analysts perform this method. Organizations use this method to assess if their products and services provide a return on investment.

Artifact

An artifact is an actual published deliverable produced by a process analyst. These can include a process model or a procedure guide. Artifacts are always stored on a process repository.

Asynchronous Process

In some BPM circles, process analysts describe an asynchronous process as one that will stop the flow of a process from reaching its completion. Process analysts associate these processes with business rules and exception events that keep a process from continuing until it has been resolved by both the customer and organization. For example, if a customer sends an e-mail to an organization, then the process cannot continue until the organization has responded to the customer with an answer to their query.

Atomic Activity

Sometimes known as a "sub-atomic" activity, these are steps in a process that cannot be broken down any further. For example, pressing a specific key on a keyboard is considered a sub-atomic activity. Process analysts will rarely model processes at this level of detail.

B

Balanced Scorecard

A performance management tool that is used by managers to measure outcomes and track the performance of both employees and business activities. Its objective is to provide managers with a standard framework that describes the objectives of each business task and allows staff to measure themselves against the scorecard. It also facilitates performance transparency and links performance to KRAs and KPIs.

Batch Processing

A series of tasks that a computer can complete without manual intervention. An example is when a computer can pay a number of invoices automatically and all at once.

Benchmarking

A method used by process analysts to assess how well a process performs in comparison to other similar processes. Benchmarking functionality can be found in workflow engine software that uses Business Activity Monitoring—where the performance of a process is watched in real time.

Blueprint

See *Roadmap.*

Business Activity Monitoring (BAM)

The aggregation, analysis, and presentation of real-time information about activities within an organization that involves customers and partners. In BPM, BAM means using computer systems that aid the monitoring of business activities.

Business Architecture

A discipline of Enterprise Architecture that focuses on corporate business, as well as the documents and diagrams that describe the architectural structure of a business. People who build business architecture are known as business architects.

Business Continuity Planning (BCP)

A formalized planning that helps organizations identify internal and external threats to their operational ability. BCP planning also involves the appropriate response measures in order for an organization to react to threats.

Business Intelligence

In BPM, business intelligence refers to the information decision makers use to improve their business. This information is usually garnered from BPM tools. However, more broadly, the term can also refer to the information an organization obtains on its competitors in order to create a competitive advantage.

Business Process

Any activity performed by an organization that starts with a customer and ends with a customer. Writing an HR policy document is not a process because it does not involve an external customer nor add any value.

Business Process Automation

In BPM, this refers to the use of BPM tools and computers to execute tasks without human intervention. Automation is key to the discipline of BPM because it ensures processes are run consistently with a high degree of predictability.

Business Process Design or Redesign

This term is no longer used in the BPM community. However, its origin stemmed from the Lean and Six Sigma discipline to describe a method of analyzing a process and changing its characteristics in order to improve it. It was made popular by academic Michael Hammer in the early 1990s. See *Business Process Reengineering.*

Business Process Execution Language (BPEL)

BPEL is a computer programming language that is used for executing processes in web-based services. It is based on XML and is the standard code used by most of the major software companies worldwide. BPEL is different from BPMN in that it does not use a visual schematic to represent processes.

Business Process Hierarchy

A product of Process Architecture, a hierarchy is the most common (and recommended) means to manage processes within an organization. It uses a set of principles and frameworks to ensure that it can be governed with minimal disruption to business activities. A Process Hierarchy uses a four-tiered classification system to delineate where processes sit in relevance to each other.

Business Process Improvement (BPI)

A generic term that is loosely used in the BPM community although it is beginning to be phased out. It refers to the discipline of analyzing a process with the aim to optimize it. Business Process Improvement is commonly associated with the Lean and Six Sigma disciplines.

Business Process Language

A generic term that is used to describe the computer code that sits behind BPEL, XML, and BPM.

Business Process Management (BPM)

The umbrella term to describe the management of business processes within an organization using a best-practice and internationally-recognized framework and methodology. BPM also implies that its responsibility extends to improving the performance of a process and, therefore, incorporates the two change management disciplines of Lean and Six Sigma.

Business Process Management Activity Cycle

Known in IT circles as a "life cycle," the BPM Activity Cycle is a process used by a center of excellence to manage and optimize business processes. The phases are broken down into eight steps and provide a process analyst with a structured approach to working with subject matter experts in developing and implementing processes within a business.

Business Process Management Initiative (BPMI)

The former trading name of the Object Management Group (OMG).

Business Process Management Suite (BPMS)

See *Workflow Engine*.

Business Process Model and Notation (BPMN)

BPMN is an international standard that is used to graphically represent a business process in a business process model. The Object Management Group manages the standard. At time of this writing, the latest version of BPMN is 2.0.

Business Process Modeling

Incorrectly abbreviated as BPM (which is reserved for Business Process Management), Business Process Modeling refers to the method a process analyst will use to visually depict the processes of a business using a dynamic modeling tool.

Business Process Modeling Tool

A software tool that allows process analysts to create dynamic process models and manage them in a repository. Modeling tools usually come with a simulation function to allow the process analyst to measure the performance of a process using data gathered from Lean and Six Sigma practitioners.

Business Process Reengineering (BPR)

Similar to Business Process Design and Business Process Improvement, the term was made popular by academic Michael Hammer in the early 1990s. Despite its title, it actually referred to the removal of manual processes (i.e., where people were utilized) as opposed to optimizing existing ones. The term is no longer used in the BPM community as it has negative connotations associated with it (people viewed it as a staff redundancy methodology). Prior to his death in 2008, Michael Hammer declared that implementation of BPR in an organization was a mistake, and people were an organization's most important asset.

Business Process Tool

A generic term that refers to any dynamic process modeling software.

Business Rules

In the context of BPM, placing rules in a process usually implies that process needs to be controlled for either assurance or risk purposes. Many BPM tools have a feature embedded that allows process analysts to prevent a process from being executed unless it has been checked by a supervisor or manager.

Business Strategy

A field that deals with the major intended and emergent initiatives taken by general managers on behalf of owners. It involves utilization of resources to enhance the performance of organizations in their external environments. It entails specifying the organization's mission, vision, and objectives; developing policies and plans (often in terms of projects and programs) designed to achieve these objectives; and allocating resources to implement those policies and plans, projects, and programs. Also known as "strategic management."

Business Unit

Any branch, team, or section within an organization that resides outside the BPM Center of Excellence.

C

Career Development Model (CDM)

Used within a BPM Center of Excellence, a CDM provides process analysts with a clear and structured approach for improving and assessing their skills as analysts and internal business consultants. The CDM also helps assess an analyst's promotion prospects. In the CDM there are three levels of process analyst. They are:

- Process analyst (Level 1)

- Process architect (Level 2)

- Senior process practitioner (Level 3)

Cause-Effect Analysis

A term to describe the discipline of Six Sigma.

Chief Executive Officer (CEO)

A CEO is the highest ranking corporate officer of an organization. An individual who is appointed as a CEO of an organization reports to its board of directors.

Chief Information Officer (CIO)

The title commonly given to the most senior executive in an enterprise responsible for the IT and computer systems that support enterprise goals.

Chief Operating Officer (COO)

A COO is a high ranking corporate officer who is responsible for the daily operation of the organization. They usually report to the highest ranking executive, the CEO.

Child Process

See *Sub-Process.*

Choke Point

In BPM, a choke point refers to a process that greatly decreases, prevents, or stops the movement of a process from continuing from one activity to another. The practice of examining a model for these types of activities is called "Choke Point Analysis." Choke points usually incur losses of both time and profit to an organization.

Class Diagram

A class diagram is a type of static structure diagram that describes the structure of a system by showing its classes, attributes, operations, and relationships among those classes. This term is used by software engineers who work with Unified Modeling Language (UML).

Client

Also known as a *stakeholder,* a client is an employee of an organization who receives services provided by the BPM CoE. Clients always work within an organization that has a BPM capability—as opposed to a customer that is external to the organization.

Cloud Computing

A cheap and effective means of using software and storage space over a large network of computers. Ensures users only have access to software and storage space as they need it.

Cloud Modeler

A BPM tool that utilizes a cloud engine for storing and managing processes. Cloud Modelers are not widely adopted by organizations due to concerns over security of privately held corporate information and potential legal ramifications.

Competitive Advantage

Defined as the strategic advantage one business entity has over its rival entities within a competitive industry. Achieving competitive advantage strengthens and positions a business better within the business environment.

Core Business Process

A Core Business Process is an essential activity that, when removed from an end-to-end process, would cause significant disruption to the operation of an organization.

Crisis Management (CM)

A term that is associated with Business Continuity Management. It is the process used by an organization to improve its situation once it has been threatened by an internal or external event.

Customer

An individual or organization that pays and organization for the provision of goods or services. They are always considered external stakeholders of an organization that has a BPM capability.

Customer Relationship Management (CRM)

A term that describes the processes implemented and used by a company to handle its contact with its customers.

D

Dashboarding

In BPM, a dashboard is a real-time user interface that shows a graphical representation of both the current status and historical performance of a process. Dashboards are used with advanced BPM automation workflow engines.

Decision Point

A Decision Point is a term that is incorrectly used by many practitioners to describe a *gateway* in a process map or process model. When a computer reads an automated task that has been modeled in BPMN, it is not allowed to make a decision on behalf of the organization. Instead, the computer must follow the sequence of processes and direct the process according to how it has been defined by the process analyst in the gateway. While Decision Points are used in flowchart diagrams, they are never used in a BPM context.

Define, Measure, Analyze, Improve, Control (DMAIC)

DMAIC is a data-driven improvement cycle used for improving, optimizing, and stabilizing business processes. The DMAIC improvement cycle is essential to the process used to drive Six Sigma projects but can be used as a framework by other disciplines as well.

Defects Per Million Opportunities (DPMO)

In Six Sigma, DPMO refers to the calculation used to measure the number of defects in a process, procedure, or service in the number of millions of opportunities. For example, if a factory produces a million toys, DPMO helps assess how many toys are produced that actually contain defects.

Defects Per Unit (DPU)

In Six Sigma, DPU refers to the average number of defects per unit. The ratio of defects to unit is the universal measure of quality.

Deming, William Edwards

An American statistician, professor, author, lecturer and consultant. He is best known for his work in Japan. From 1950 onwards, he taught top management in Japan how to improve design (and thus service), product quality, testing, and sales (the last through global markets) through various methods, including the application of statistical methods.

Department of Defense Architecture Framework (DoDAF)

An enterprise architecture framework developed by the United States Department of Defense that defines a set of views that act as mechanisms for visualizing, understanding, and assimilating the broad scope and complexities of an architecture description through tabular, structural, behavioral, and graphical means.

Diagram

In BPM, a diagram refers to a static map that, when developed, cannot be altered or manipulated any further. Process analysts will usually develop diagrams for presentation purposes only.

Differentiation

A concept used in business strategy that describes one of three ways to establish a competitive advantage. Differentiation advantage occurs when a firm delivers greater services for a lower price than its competitors.

E

End-to-end

A process that starts with the customer and ends with the customer. When a process analyst states they're developing an end-to-end process model it means they will look at the entire spectrum of all attributes associated with that process.

Enterprise Architecture

The process of translating business vision and strategy into effective enterprise change by creating, communicating, and improving key requirements, principles, and models that describe the enterprise's future state and enable its evolution. In the change management industry, Enterprise Architecture is considered a sub-discipline of Business Strategy.

Enterprise Resource Planning (ERP)

ERP describes systems used to integrate internal and external management information across an entire organization. ERP should embrace finance/ accounting, manufacturing, sales and service, and customer relationship management. ERP systems automate this activity with an integrated software application. In BPM, most automation workflow engines are ERP systems.

Extensible Markup Language (XML)

A computer language that defines a set of rules for encoding documents in a format that is both human-readable and machine-readable. It is defined in the XML 1.0 specification produced by the W3C, and several other related specifications. The design goals of XML emphasize simplicity, generality, and usability over the Internet. It is a textual data format with strong support via Unicode for the languages of the world. Although the design of XML focuses on documents, it is widely used for the representation of arbitrary data structures, for example, in web services.

F

Full Time Equivalent (FTE)

FTE is a unit that indicates the workload of an employed person in a way that makes workloads comparable across various contexts. FTE is often used to measure a worker's involvement in a project or to track cost reductions in an organization.

Function

A series of high-level processes that, when combined, form the entire value chain of an organization. For example, "sales" is considered a function whereas "receive customer order" is considered a process.

Functional Decomposition Diagram

A method used by process analysts to list all activities in an end-to-end process before actually modeling them in a BPM tool. The diagrams are usually populated in an excel spreadsheet and list the process owner, hierarchy number, and description of each process. This enables the process analyst to verify all processes with a subject matter expert before representing them in a model—which can be very time intensive.

Function Model

A functional model, also called an activity model, is a graphical representation of an enterprise's function within a defined scope. The purposes of a function model are to describe the functions and processes, assist with the discovery of information needs, identify opportunities, and establish a basis for determining product and service cost. Business architects create these artifacts.

G

Gap Analysis

A tool that helps process analysts compare the actual performance of a process with its potential performance.

Gateway

In BPMN, a gateway is a notation used to control how sequence flows interact as they converge and diverge within a process. Process analysts generally use four types of gateways when modeling. They are exclusive, inclusive, complex, and parallel gateways. All types of gateways are represented using a diamond shape.

Governance

The third pillar within the business layer of a BPM Center of Excellence. Governance consists of the methodology and approach a center of excellence uses to manage processes across the enterprise and to ensure that it retains all control of the ownership of process artifacts. Without the governance pillar, an organization is not considered to have a BPM capability.

H

Hammer, Michael

An American engineer, business management author, and a former professor of computer science at the Massachusetts Institute of Technology (MIT); known as one of the founders of the management theory of Business Process Reengineering (BPR).

Harrington, James

An American author, engineer, entrepreneur, and consultant in performance improvement. Over his career he developed many concepts, including poor-quality cost and business process improvement.

I

IDEF

IDEF was first adopted by the United States Air Force in 1970. It is a methodology used to model the functions within an organization and offers a modeling language for the analysis, development, re-engineering, and integration of information systems, a business process, or software analysis.

Information Technology (IT)

A branch of engineering that deals with the use of computers and telecommunications to store, retrieve, and transmit information.

Information, Communications and Technology (ICT)

A reference to IT that includes the communications component. Specifically, it refers to the technology behind technologies such as satellites and VoIP.

International Standards Organization (ISO)

An international standard-setting body composed of representatives that promulgate world wide proprietary, industrial, and commercial standards.

Intranet

A computer network that uses Internet technology to share information, operational systems, or computing services within an organization.

J

Job Description

A document that lists the tasks, roles, and responsibilities of a position. It may include information on qualifications and/or skills required, a reporting structure, salary range to key performance measurements, and bonuses.

Juran, Joseph

A management consultant who is principally remembered as an evangelist for quality and quality management; wrote several influential books on those subjects.

Just In Time (JIT)

A strategy that organizations utilize to increase efficiency and reduce waste by receiving goods and services only as they are required in the process, resulting in a reduction in holding costs.

K

Kanban

A Lean manufacturing term that literally means "signboard" or "billboard." It is a scheduling system that helps determine what to produce, when to produce it, and how much to produce.

Knowledge Management

Practices and processes designed to identify, capture, leverage, disseminate, and share an organization's intellectual assets to deliver value.

Key Result Area (KRA)

A key result area generally refers to the outcomes or outputs that either a department or individual is responsible for.

Key Performance Indicator (KPI)

A type of performance measurement that is used by an organization to evaluate its success or the success of a particular activity. However, KPIs can be attached to all levels of the organization, including individual staff members. In BPM, KPIs are attached to each activity within an end-to-end process model.

L

Lean Manufacturing

A sub-discipline of BPM that considers the expenditure of resources for any goal other than the creation of value for the end customer to be wasteful, and thus a target for elimination. Working from the perspective of the customer who consumes a product or service, "value" is defined as any action or process that a customer would be willing to pay for.

Lean Six Sigma

Lean Six Sigma is a term invented by author Michael George in 2002 as a means to describe a combined managerial concept of both Lean and Six Sigma. Although Lean and Six Sigma are two different disciplines, they are often incorrectly referred to as a single change management function as they both examine results for the elimination of waste using slightly similar methodologies and tools. The correct description is "Lean *and* Six Sigma."

Levels of Analysis

There are three main levels used to conduct a strategic analysis of an organization. The first level is the operating environment. The value chains within the business follow it in the second level. The third level is people and systems that perform each function with the cost and time associated to each activity.

M

Management Consulting

Refers to the practice of helping organizations improve their performance, primarily through the analysis of existing organizational problems and development of plans for improvement. Organizations may draw upon the services of management consultants for a number of reasons, including gaining external (and presumably objective) advice and access to the consultants' specialized expertise.

Measure

The process or result of determining the ratio of a physical quantity (such as length, time, temperature, etc.) to a unit of measure, such as the meter, second, or degree Celsius.

Measures Hierarchy

A hierarchical tree that indicates the specific measures for processes, sub processes, and activities within an organization.

Metadata

An ambiguous term used for two fundamentally different concepts (types). Although the expression "data about data" is often used, it does not apply to both in the same way. Structural metadata (the design and specification of data structures) cannot be about data because at design time the application contains no data. In this case, the correct description would be "data about the containers of data." Descriptive metadata, on the other hand, is about individual instances of application data—the data content. In this case, a useful description (resulting in a disambiguating neologism) would be "data about data content" or "content about content," thus meta content.

Middleware

Software that functions as an integrator or exchange layer between two or more software applications.

Model Driven Architecture (MDA)

A software design approach for the development of software systems. It provides a set of guidelines for the structuring of specifications, which are expressed as models.

N

Non-Value Adding Activities

A Lean manufacturing term that describes an activity that is wasteful, doesn't add value, or is unproductive. It is also a key concept in the Toyota Production System and is one of the three types of waste (muda, mura, muri). Waste reduction is an effective way to increase profitability.

O

Object Management Group (OMG)

An international consortium, originally aimed at setting standards for distributed object-oriented systems, now focused on modeling (programs, systems, and business processes) and model-based standards.

Operational Level Agreement (OLA)

An OLA defines the interdependent relationships among the internal support groups of an organization working to support a service-level agreement (SLA). The agreement describes the responsibilities of each internal support group toward other support groups, including the process and timeframe for delivery of their services. The objective of the OLA is to present a clear, concise, and measurable description of the service provider's internal support relationships.

Organization

Refers to a legal entity corporation that has been set up with the view to sell goods or services.

Organization Chart

A diagram that shows the structure of an organization including the relationships and relative ranks of its parts and positions/jobs. The term is also used for similar diagrams, for example, diagrams showing the different elements of a field of knowledge or a group of languages.

Outsourcing

The process of contracting an existing business function or process to an independent organization and ceasing to perform that function or process internally. Instead, it is purchased as a service. Though this practice of purchasing a business function—instead of providing it internally—is a common feature of any modern economy, the term outsourcing became popular in America near the turn of the twenty-first century. An outsourcing deal may also involve transfer of the employees involved to the outsourcing business partner.

P

Parent Process

A term to describe any process that contains a number of child or sub-processes. It can also mean it is located at a higher level within the Business Process Hierarchy. See *Sub-processes*.

Performance

Generically refers to activities that ensure goals are consistently being met in an effective and efficient manner. Performance management can focus on the performance of an organization, a department, employee, or even the processes to build a product or service, as well as many other areas.

Poka-Yoke

A Lean manufacturing term that means creating a "fail-safe" or "mistake-proof" mechanism. A poka-yoke is any method in a Lean manufacturing process that helps an equipment operator "avoid" (yokeru) "mistakes" (poka). Its purpose is to eliminate product defects by preventing, correcting, or drawing attention to human errors as they occur.

Portal

Also known as an *enterprise* or *intranet* portal, a portal is the gateway that unifies access to all enterprise information and applications on an intranet. It is a tool that helps a company manage its data, applications, and information more easily through personalized views. Some portal solutions today are able to integrate legacy applications, other portals objects, and handle thousands of user requests.

Process Analyst

A generic term used to describe a full time BPM practitioner. The term Process Analyst can also be used to reference a process architect or senior practitioner. A process analyst is someone who has industry recognized qualifications in either BPM, Lean, or Six Sigma. However, the Lean and Six Sigma disciplines use a color belt system to identify that someone has achieved a particular level of accreditation (e.g., Green Belt).

Process Architecture (Business Process Architecture)

The structural design of general process systems that applies to fields such as computers (software, hardware, networks, etc.), business processes (enterprise architecture, policy and procedures, logistics, project management, etc.), and any other process system of varying degrees of complexity. In BPM, Process Architecture refers to the design of process categorization according to the functions performed by an organization. The output of process architecture is a Business Process Hierarchy.

Procedure Guide

A textual representation of an end-to-end process that is usually developed by a dynamic BPM tool. Procedure guides are used for training and auditing purposes to help employees understand how a process is executed. However, they are rarely relied upon as being the source of truth for a process. As a result, procedure guides are developed after a process model has been created.

Process Map

A flat file representation of a process that, once developed, cannot be altered or manipulated in any way. Process maps are typically developed using static BPM tools such as Power Point, Word, or Visio.

Process Model

A representation of an end-to-end process that is developed using a dynamic BPM tool. Process models allow analysts to manage large volumes of activities and run simulation events to identify areas in a process that can be optimized.

Process Repository

A database that houses all process artifacts. Repositories are created using a process architecture numbering system that allows employees of an organization to identify a logical correlation between parent and child processes. Repositories are the responsibility of a BPM Center of Excellence and contain process models and procedure guides. They are managed using a dynamic BPM tool.

Process Steward

An employee of an organization who does not work in a BPM Center of Excellence but has been given the responsibility to act as their representative in their respective business unit. Process stewards are critical to successful governance as they act as the conduit between the business units and the center of excellence. Process stewards are responsible for ensuring all process models in their line of business are maintained and managed according to the organization's governance structure.

Product

A product is a thing that is produced by labor or effort. In business, a customer uses it to describe the production of an item that satisfies a need or a want.

R

RACI Matrix

Describes the participation by various roles in completing tasks or deliverables for a project or business process. It is especially useful in clarifying roles and responsibilities in cross-functional/departmental projects and processes. It is an acronym for Responsible, Accountable, Consulted, Informed.

Reference Model

An abstract framework or domain-specific ontology consisting of an inter-linked set of clearly-defined concepts produced by an expert or body of experts in order to encourage clear communication. A reference model can represent the component parts of any consistent idea, from business functions to system components, as long as it represents a complete set. This frame of reference can then be used to communicate ideas clearly among members of the same community. Reference models are often illustrated as a set of concepts with some indication of the relationships between the concepts.

Roadmap

Refers to a comprehensive plan detailing the activities required by an organization to go from one state to another. It lists both the set of activities and the indicative date the organization expects to achieve those activities. In BPM, a roadmap is developed by the BPM Center of Excellence and describes how the team will implement process management across the organization.

S

Sarbanes-Oxley Act

A United States federal law that set new or enhanced standards for all US public company boards, management, and public accounting firms. The bill was enacted as a reaction to a number of major corporate and accounting scandals including those affecting Enron, Tyco International, Adelphia, Peregrine Systems, and WorldCom. These scandals, which cost investors billions of dollars when the share prices of the affected companies collapsed, shook public confidence in the nation's securities markets.

Service

In the context of enterprise architecture, the term service refers to a set of related software functionalities that can be reused for different purposes with the policies that should control its usage. However, in a business context, a service is an economic activity where the buyer does not, except by exclusive contract, obtain exclusive ownership of the thing purchased. The benefits of such a service, if priced, are held to be self-evident in the buyer's willingness to pay for it. Public services are those society as a whole pays for through taxes and other means.

Service Catalogue

A list of services that an organization provides (often to its employees or customers) that is managed and housed in a repository.

Service Level Agreement (SLA)

Part of a service contract that formally defines the level of service. In practice, the term SLA is sometimes used to refer to the contracted delivery time (of the service) or performance. As an example, Internet service providers will commonly include service level agreements within the terms of their contracts with customers to define the level(s) of service being sold in plain language terms. In this case, the SLA will typically have a technical definition in terms of mean time between failures (MTBF), mean time to repair or mean time to recovery (MTTR), various data rates, throughput, jitter, or similar measurable details.

Service Oriented Architecture

A set of principles and methodologies for designing and developing software in the form of interoperable services. These services are well-defined business functionalities that are built as software components (discrete pieces of code and/or data structures) that can be reused for different purposes. SOA design principles are used during the phases of systems development and integration.

Simulation

A technique used to imitate the operation of a real-world process or system over time. The act of simulating something first requires that a model be developed; this model represents the key characteristics or behaviors of the selected physical or abstract system or process. The model represents the system itself, whereas the simulation represents the operation of the system over time.

SIPOC

SIPOC is a Six Sigma tool used in phase one or the "Define Phase" of the DMAIC process to gather information about any process. It is an acronym for Supplier, Input, Process, Output, Customer.

Six Sigma

Six Sigma is a sub-discipline of BPM that seeks to improve the quality of process outputs by identifying and removing the causes of defects (errors) and minimizing variability in manufacturing and business processes. It uses a set of quality management methods, including statistical methods, and creates a special infrastructure of people within the organization ("Black Belts," "Green Belts," etc.) who are experts in these methods. Each Six Sigma project carried out within an organization follows a defined sequence of steps and has quantified financial targets (cost reduction and/or profit increase).

Software Requirements

A requirements specification for a software system—is a complete description of the behavior of a system to be developed. It includes a set of use cases that describe all the interactions the users will have with the software. In addition to use cases, the specification also contains non-functional requirements. Non-functional requirements are requirements that impose constraints on the design or implementation (such as performance engineering requirements, quality standards, or design constraints).

Steering Group

A committee established to oversee the implementation of BPM within an organization. Its responsibility is to monitor the progress of each implementation activity and be accountable for the success of the project. Steering Groups should only be comprised of the most senior executives within an organization such as the COO, CIO, Manager of CoE and other affected key stakeholders.

Strategy

A plan of action designed to achieve a vision. In a business context, "strategy" is developed at the highest level of an organization and sets the future agenda. It is developed by business strategy analysts and shared with the organization through blueprints or roadmaps.

Subject Matter Expert (SME)

Also known as a *domain* expert, an SME is person who is an expert in a particular area or topic. When spoken, sometimes the acronym "SME" is spelled out ("S-M-E") and at other times pronounced as a word ("smee"). A domain expert is a person with special knowledge or skills in a particular area of endeavor. An accountant is an expert in the domain of accountancy, for example. The development of accounting software requires knowledge in two different domains, namely accounting and software. Some of the development workers may be experts in one domain and not the other.

Sub-Processes

There are four levels within a Business Process Hierarchy and each level represents a layer of detail within a process. Process analysts refer to a sub-process as being the next level of detail down within an end-to-end business process. For example, "make coffee" is considered a sub-process of "sell coffee" because selling a cup of coffee to a customer incorporates a whole number of separate processes of which making the coffee is a specific part. Sub-processes are also known as "child processes" because, in a hierarchy type structure, they are subordinate to a higher level process.

Supply Chain Management

The management of a network of interconnected businesses involved in the ultimate provision of product and service packages required by end customers. Supply chain management spans all movement and storage of raw materials, work-in-process inventory, and finished goods from point of origin to point of consumption (supply chain).

Swim Lane

In BPMN, swim lanes are a visual mechanism for organizing and categorizing activities based on cross-functional flowcharting. In BPMN, it consists of two types:

- **Pool:** Represents major participants in a process, typically separating different organizations. A pool contains one or more lanes (like a real swimming pool). A pool can be open (i.e., showing internal detail) when it is depicted as a large rectangle showing one or more lanes, or collapsed (i.e., hiding internal detail) when it is depicted as an empty rectangle stretching the width or length of the diagram.

- **Lane:** Used to organize and categorize activities within a pool according to function or role, and depicted as a rectangle stretching the width or length of the pool. A lane contains the flow objects, connecting objects and artifacts.

System

In BPM, a system is a term to describe the IT capability of an organization. It refers to when software, hardware, and people are combined together to produce an IT-based outcome.

T

The Open Group Architecture Framework (TOGAF)

A framework for enterprise architecture that provides a comprehensive approach for designing, planning, implementation, and governance of an enterprise information architecture. TOGAF is a high level and holistic approach to design, which is typically modeled at four levels: Business, Application, Data, and Technology. It tries to give a well-tested overall starting model to information architects, which can then be built upon. It relies heavily on modularization, standardization, and already existing, proven technologies and products.

Timeclocking

This tool is categorized as a sub-component of both simulation and dashboarding. Timeclocking is essentially the discipline of measuring how long it takes to complete a process. The benefit of time clocking is so that process analysts can pinpoint exactly where the "chokepoints" are in an end-to-end sequence flow.

Total Cycle Time

The total amount of time it takes to produce a product or service from end to end. Process analysts will calculate this time by adding the sum of all cycle times of each activity that equates to the total cycle time.

Total Quality Management (TQM)

A movement, an industrial discipline, and a set of techniques for improving the quality of processes. TQM emphasizes constant measures and statistical techniques to help improve and then maintain the output quality of processes. TQM is often associated with William Edwards Deming who championed the concept.

Toyota Production System (TPS)

The Toyota Production System (TPS) is an integrated socio-technical system developed by Toyota that comprises its management philosophy and practices. The TPS organizes manufacturing and logistics for the automobile manufacturer, including interaction with suppliers and customers. The system is a major precursor of the more generic "lean manufacturing."

Transaction Processing

In computer science, transaction processing is information processing that is divided into individual, indivisible operations called transactions. Each transaction must succeed or fail as a complete unit; it cannot remain in an intermediate state.

U

UML (Unified Modeling Language)

A standardized general-purpose modeling language in the field of object-oriented software engineering. The standard is managed, and was created, by the Object Management Group. UML was first added to the list of OMG adopted technologies in 1997 and has since become the industry standard for modeling software-intensive systems.

Use Case Diagram

A use case diagram, at its simplest, is a graphical representation of a user's interaction with the system and depicts the specifications of a use case. A use case diagram can portray the different types of users of a system and the various ways that they interact with the system. This type of diagram is typically used in conjunction with the textual use case and will often be accompanied by other types of diagrams as well.

V

Value Added Activity

A process or activity that adds value to a product or service is called a "value-added activity." Value is judged by the customer, who can be the customer of the company, or an internal customer who receives the output of the process or activity. An activity or process adds value, if it satisfies all three of these requirements: (1) the customer is willing to pay for the process or activity, (2) the process or activity physically changes or transforms the process or activity, and (3) the process or activity is performed correctly the first time it's undertaken.

Value Chain

A value chain is a chain of activities for an organization operating in a specific industry. The business unit is the appropriate level for construction of a value chain, not the divisional level or corporate level. Products pass through all activities of the chain in order, and at each activity the product gains some value. The chain of activities gives the products more added value than the sum of the independent activities' values. A diamond cutter, as a profession, can be used to illustrate the difference of cost and the value chain. The cutting activity may have a low cost, but the activity adds much of the value to the end product (a rough diamond is significantly less valuable than a cut diamond). Typically, the described value chain and the documentation of processes, assessment and auditing of adherence to the process routines are at the core of the quality certification of the business.

W

Web Services

A vague term that refers to distributed or virtual applications or processes that use the Internet to link activities or software components. A travel web site that takes a reservation from a customer, and then sends a message to a hotel application (accessed via the web) to determine if a room is available, books it, and tells the customer he or she has a reservation is an example of a Web Services application.

Workflow

A generic term that refers to a sequence of connected steps.

Workflow Engine

In BPM, a workflow engine is a software application that manages and executes modeled computer processes (usually using BPMN). It is a key component in workflow technology and typically makes use of a database server. A workflow engine interprets events, such as documents submitted to a server or due dates expiring, and acts on them according to defined computer processes. The actions may be anything from saving the document in a document management system, issuing new work by sending an e-mail to users, or escalating overdue work items to management. A workflow engine facilitates the flow of information, tasks, and events. Workflow engines may also be referred to as a Workflow Orchestration Engines or Business Process Management Suites.

Workflow Model

A workflow model is a term used by process analysts to describe a process model that has been solely developed to be applied to a Workflow Engine. It means it has been developed in BPMN and uses XML to execute processes that have been identified for automation.

X

XML

See *Extensible Markup Language.*

Z

Zachman Framework

An Enterprise Architecture framework for enterprise architecture that provides a formal and highly structured way of viewing and defining an enterprise. It consists of a two dimensional classification matrix based on the intersection of six communication questions (What, Where, When, Why, Who and How) with six rows according to reification transformations.

Zachman, John

An American business and IT consultant who is credited as being the early pioneer of enterprise architecture. He is the Chief Executive Officer of Zachman International, and originator of the Zachman Framework.

THE EXPERT'S CORNER

At this point, you should have a high-level understanding of the following:

- Key terminologies associated with BPM

Chapter 8

EXAMPLE OF A BPM CERTIFICATION EXAM

What you will learn in this section:

- Be provided with a sample certification exam that you can provide your staff

- Answers are highlighted in **bold** text

About This Exam

The purpose of this exam is to test your understanding of the basic concepts behind Business Process Management.

All questions contained in this exam directly relate to the function of a business process analyst within a center of excellence.

Successful completion of this exam will lead to becoming a certified BPM process analyst.

In order to pass this exam you need to achieve a score of **70 percent** or higher.

You have **90 minutes** to complete the exam.

Your name:

_____

SECTION A: FUNDAMENTAL BPM AND PROCESS MODELING

The following questions relate to the basic discipline of BPM and Process Modeling. Circle the correct answer or write the answer where required.

1. A Business Process is…

a) Any set of tasks performed by a business that form a sequence flow

b) Any set of activities performed by a business to form a sequence flow

c) **Any set of activities performed by a business that is initiated by an event**

d) Any set of events performed by a business that depict an end-to-end function

2. A Value Chain is…

a) A diagram used to measure value within an organization

b) A series of events that highlights the value to an organization

c) A model for identifying logistics operations within a business

d) **A chain of activities for a firm operating in a specific industry**

3. A workflow model is…

a) A process model that depicts systems

b) **A process map that depicts both people and systems**

c) An executable process model that facilitates automation

d) A process model that depicts a sequence of events between systems

4. An Activity is...

a) **A process that can be sub-divided into small units or sub-processes**

b) A series of high-level events that occur within a business

c) A sub-set of process tasks

d) A set of processes that have been modeled and optimized

5. The first step of the BPM Activity Cycle is...

a) Design

b) **Define**

c) Execute

d) Analyze

6. Name three attributes you are likely to find in a superior process

a) _____

b) _____

c) _____

Answer: Maximizes value and eliminates waste, has a documented design, is simple and flexible, compresses time, provides real-time feedback, has clear links to other processes, adds value to the customer, and is user friendly and repeatable.

7. Name three commonly used mapping tools

a) _____

b) _____

c) _____

Answer: Any answer that describes a static tool will be accepted. Answers include post-it notes, butcher paper, Microsoft Word, Visio or Excel

8. To determine the position of a process in terms of depth and sequence, a process analyst can use...

a) A dynamic process repository

b) A modeling tool

c) A process taxonomy

d) **Numbering standards**

9. A customer has failed to fill in a field within an application form. As a result, the process cannot continue. In BPM, this is an example of...

a) An end point

b) **An exit point**

c) A process exception

d) An incomplete output

SECTION B: THE BPM CENTER OF EXCELLENCE

The following questions relate to the BPM Center of Excellence.

Circle the correct answer.

10. Services a BPM Center of Excellence should provide its customers are:

a) **Simulation, Dashboarding, Timeclocking, and Cost Benefit Analysis**

b) Chokepoint analysis, Timeclocking, Simulation, and Cost Benefit Analysis

c) Cost Benefit Analysis, Customer Benefit Analysis, Simulation, and Dashboarding

d) Timeclocking, Process Modeling, Simulation, and Dashboarding

11. The business process hierarchy is broken into classes. In order, they are...

a) Process, Activity, Process Group, Category

b) Process Group, Category, Activity, Process

c) Activity, Process, Process Group, Category

d) **Category, Process Group, Process, Activity**

12. The purpose of the business process hierarchy is to...

a) Develop a process repository that will align with business architecture frameworks

b) Segregate process models from procedure guides

c) Align the categorization of process models using the same framework as other financial institutions

d) **Categorize each process model using a best practice framework**

13. The role of a BPM Center of Excellence is to...

a) **Discover and assist with the governance and improvement of business processes**

b) Use notation and modeling techniques that align with international standards

c) Re-engineer processes for high-level architecture viewpoints

d) Assist stakeholders with their process modeling activities

14. According to the BPM Center of Excellence, a process stakeholder is…

a) A single conduit that represents one of the nine business lines

b) A staff member who is employed within the BPM team

c) **A team or individual who resides outside the direct reporting chain of the process steward**

d) A person who has requested a task through the BPM workbench

15. A process analyst is responsible for…

a) Developing end-to-end process models

b) Ensuring process models meet compliance requirements

c) Ensuring process models are aligned with enterprise architecture viewpoints

d) **Saving the organization costs in terms of time and money**

SECTION C: BUSINESS ARCHITECTURE

The following questions relate to the practice of business architecture.

Circle the correct answer or write the answer where required.

16. The business architecture team's equivalent of BPMN is…

a) UML

b) **Archimate**

c) BPEL

d) XML

17. Examples of business architecture frameworks include...

a) DoDAF

b) Zachman

c) TOGAF

d) **All of the above**

18. A method used by business architects for developing artifacts is the...

a) **Architecture Development Method**

b) Target Architecture Development Method

c) Architecture Development Cycle

d) Artifact Development Method

19. Name three kinds of advantages that are built as a result of business architecture...

a) _____

b) _____

c) _____

Answers: corporate alignment, business design, change management facilitation, gap analysis, value chain analysis, organization re-engineering

20. SOA stands for...

a) Software-oriented architecture

b) Solution-oriented architecture

c) **Service-oriented architecture**

d) System-oriented architecture

SECTION D: CLIENT ENGAGEMENT

The following questions relate to how the CoE should engage its clients.

Circle the correct answer or write the answer where required.

21. The four comparable components of the BPM Activity Cycle are...

a) Receive Request, Process Data, Model Data, Publish Project

b) **Forward Request, Collect Data, Process Data, Disseminate Project**

c) Forward Request, Analyze Data, Model Data, Disseminate Project

d) Receive Request, Analyze Data, Model Process, Publish Project

22. A recommended limit for the number of people participating in a workshop is...

a) 5

b) **10**

c) 15

d) 20

23. In any organization, the recommended number of analysts attending a client interview should be...

a) **Two business process analysts**

b) A single business process analyst

c) Two business process architects

d) A senior process analyst and a note taker

24. Name three types of information you should attempt to obtain when meeting with customers in either a workshop or interview

a) _____

b) _____

c) _____

Answers: organization chart, objectives of the process, customer of the process, input and output of the process, how to improve the process, relationships between different departments, service level agreements

25. A client has requested the development of a new procedure guide. The first thing a process analyst must do is...

a) Develop a stakeholder engagement plan

b) Conduct stakeholder interviews then commence writing the guide

c) Check if an older procedure guide exists

d) **Check if an end-to-end completed process model in BPMN exists**

26. A client has asked a process model to be changed. The first thing you must do is...

a) **Obtain details about the process change including the benefit it will provide to the organization**

b) Ensure the request has been submitted into the workbench

c) Start the modeling process

d) Speak to the business process manager representing the business unit to gain their approval

27. A business process analyst has the right to refuse a task from a client that does not result in a benefit to the organization

a) **True**

b) False

SECTION E: FUNDAMENTAL BPMN RULES AND PRINCIPLES

The following questions relate to BPMN rules and principles.

Circle the correct answer.

28. The first thing a process analyst must do when creating a model is…

a) Identify the main activities and decision points

b) **Determine the beginning and end points**

c) Order and link the activities and decision points

d) Decompose activities only as needed

29. OLA stands for…

a) Organizational Level Agreement

b) Organizational Level Architecture

c) Operational Level Architecture

d) **Operational Level Agreement**

30. A start event can have an error trigger

a) True

b) **False**

c) Depends on the process

31. An end event cannot have an outgoing sequence flow

a) **True**

b) False

c) Depends on the process

32. A sequence flow cannot cross a pool or sub process boundary

a) **True**

b) False

c) Depends on the process

33. Two activities in the same process can have the same name

a) True

b) False

c) **Depends on the process**

34. A Functional Decomposition Diagram is...

a) An architecture catalogue which allows process analysts to view process traceability across an organization

b) A use-case model that depicts the functional dependencies between processes

c) **A top-down approach to process analysis starting from organization processes at the highest level**

d) A diagram that lists all process models in a repository so that process analysts can assess process duplication

35. The highest level of a process measurement is...

a) Strategic outcomes

b) Enterprise outcomes

c) Business outcomes

d) **Organizational outcomes**

36. A KPI is…

a) **A technique used to evaluate success of a particular activity**

b) An executable trigger that advises management that an activity is successful

c) A technique used to evaluate success and failure of a particular activity

d) An executable trigger that advises management that an activity is both successful and unsuccessful

37. An example of a differentiator is…

a) Achieving process automation through the establishment of a workflow engine

b) Conducting end-to-end process modeling to achieve business optimization

c) **Personalized customer service**

d) Successful application of enterprise architecture across an organization

SECTION F: BPM NOTATION

Write the name of the notation next to each of these symbols.

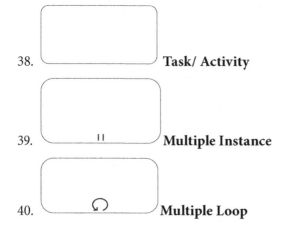

38. **Task/ Activity**

39. **Multiple Instance**

40. **Multiple Loop**

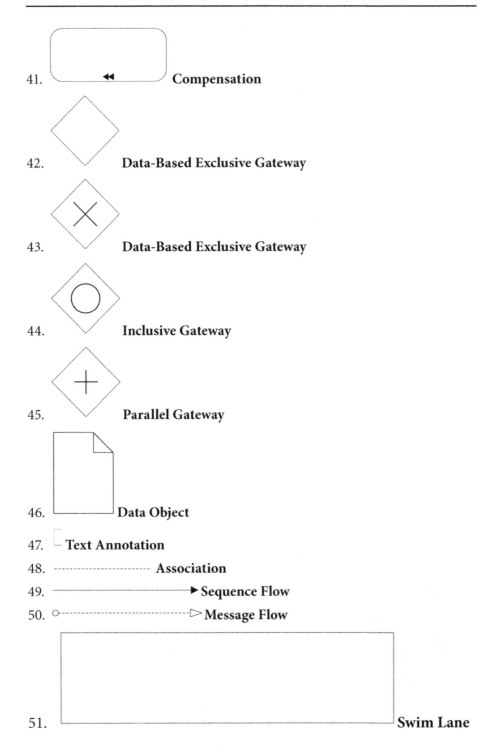

41. Compensation

42. Data-Based Exclusive Gateway

43. Data-Based Exclusive Gateway

44. Inclusive Gateway

45. Parallel Gateway

46. Data Object

47. Text Annotation

48. Association

49. Sequence Flow

50. Message Flow

51. Swim Lane

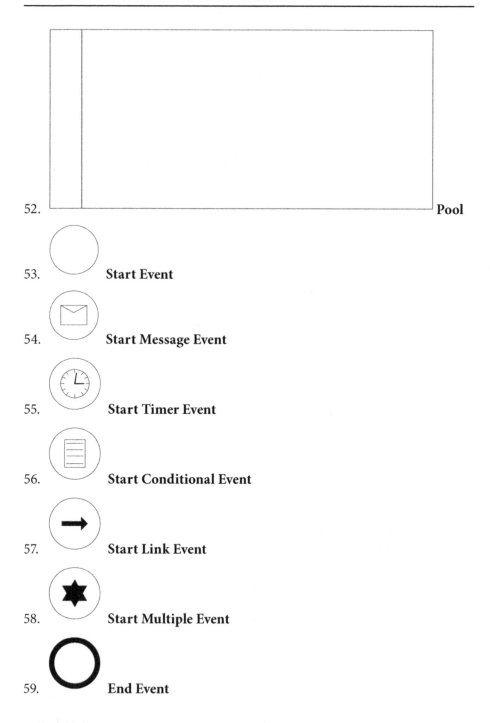

52. **Pool**

53. Start Event

54. Start Message Event

55. Start Timer Event

56. Start Conditional Event

57. Start Link Event

58. Start Multiple Event

59. End Event

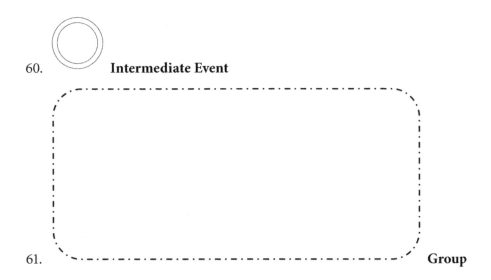

60.   **Intermediate Event**

61.   **Group**

Chapter 9

BRINGING IT ALL TOGETHER

Now that you've read this book, it's time to get to work and translate all your learning into action. What I've discussed has provided you with a high-level view of each aspect of BPM. But in reality, each chapter could have an entire book devoted to it. For example, the "process" pillar of BPM can be very technical depending on the complexity of the organization where you work. I've also personally spent many months just working on the "People" aspect of BPM—because some organizations realize they don't have any policies in place to create an environment of "process culture" among their staff.

Above all, it's important to remember that there have been countless numbers of organizations that have successfully implemented BPM. Have you wondered why large organizations such as Shell, Toyota, or General Electric always seem to survive unpredictable fluctuations in the global market? It's no secret these organizations all adopted a process improvement methodology that helped reduce cost and improve efficiency. However, in the public domain, much of their success is perceived to have been attributed to either Lean or Six Sigma. It is rare that BPM is mentioned as the sole contributing factor to an organization's growth and prosperity. Few people will realize that nearly all organizations that used either Lean or Six Sigma already had a strong process management framework in place before they started tinkering with their business. It is a recognized fact that 80 percent of the world's top performing organizations manage processes using the frameworks and methodologies found in this book.

If an organization seeks long term sustainability in a volatile market, it should always first look at continuous improvement and business transformation disciplines such as BPM before thinking of any other approach. Establishing a BPM CoE will provide the organization with the flexibility to adapt in a dynamic marketplace and provide continuous improvement to its business. This has been a proven approach that large organizations such as BP, Coca Cola, and Zappos.com have adopted in order to stay one step ahead of their competitors.

If you work in a large organization and have been put in charge of implementing BPM, then my recommendation is to start with developing a business case before doing anything else. In this document you should discuss the need for a BPM CoE and list the numerous benefits that results from having a dedicated process analysis capability. This business case should always be signed off and endorsed by the most senior person in the organization. Once this is done, I'd begin to look at each of the four pillars—starting with "People" first in order to build the right team. A good manager with a poor team will never succeed. It's important to hire the right people who will champion BPM throughout the rest of the organization.

As you begin to build the practice, try to avoid some of the common pitfalls I listed in Chapter 2. Some describe process management as a long journey; however, I'd argue that BPM could be implemented very quickly if you're aware of the many hot spots that may arise. Resistance will come at you from every direction. But if you have executive endorsement (which you should), then you won't have to worry about working hard to convince others of the importance of BPM. Alternatively, you could simply hand them a copy of this book.

Lastly, always point out that all the information contained in this book is standard international best practice. Try and abstain from developing your own BPM frameworks and methodologies, as there's no need. And don't forget to highlight to your peers that successful global organizations are already using what's been discussed in this book. *That's the reason why they're successful.* From the outset, they were able to drive and manage their business rather than let market conditions dictate how they'd perform.

Chapter 10

ONE FINAL THING BEFORE YOU GO...

Once again, I'd like to thank you for buying this book and taking the time to read it. I'm sure that once you've started implementing some of the practical advice offered in this book, you'll quickly start to see positive changes in your organization. Implementing BPM is not difficult and shouldn't take a lot of time. And I also hope you found the information in this book easy to understand and easy to remember. If not, I've deliberately laid out the content of each chapter using a simple structure so if you ever get stuck, you'll be able to quickly find the right information.

As someone who advocates continuous improvement, it would be wrong of me not to seek your opinion on this book. I'd be very interested to hear from you and the types of challenges you faced when implementing BPM in your organization. If I get enough feedback then I'll certainly aim to publish a newer edition that includes your advice and personal experiences. You can contact me by logging on to www.ultimateguidetobpm.com or via my author page on Amazon.com.

But before you go, here are some other things you could also do:

1. Help promote the discipline of BPM by telling your work colleagues and managers about this book. Highlight how this book provides the necessary advice on creating a BPM capability. Tell them of the cost and time that will be saved across the organization if the frameworks and methodologies found in this book are implemented. If you're a business student in an academic institution, then please ask your professor if this book can become part of the course curriculum. BPM is very much at the center of every business, and it would be surprising to hear if it's not a core subject in any of the business courses offered.

2. Help others improve their knowledge of BPM by discussing this book on blogs, forums, and through social media. If you see any mistakes on an existing blog or website, ask the author to correct it by citing a specific page in this book. Likewise, help me educate people about BPM by improving the entries on collaborative sites such as Wikipedia.org using the correct information.

3. Log on to Amazon.com and provide feedback on this book by giving it a star rating as well as an overview of what you liked or disliked. Again, all feedback is valuable. If necessary, I'll aim to incorporate your feedback into a second edition.

4. Add tags to your Amazon.com review so that others will be able to find this book. Tags make the searching process easier plus they demonstrate that this book includes the right information as advertised. Tags include:

- BPM
- Business Process Management
- Business Process Modeling
- Business Process
- Process Management
- Business Management
- Process Maturity
- Business
- BPMN
- Lean
- Six Sigma
- Lean Six Sigma

If you find that these tags already exist on the Amazon.com listing for this book, then I'd simply ask you click on them to verify that the tags are actually associated with the content in this book.

ABOUT THE AUTHOR

Theodore Panagacos is a former Management Consultant with Booz & Company and has ten years of experience helping organizations design and implement business models that improve services to customers. He has a strong background in business optimization and performance measurement, and has worked across a range of functional areas relating to ICT transformation, business strategy, project management, corporate governance reform, and organizational re-engineering. He works and resyides in Melbourne, Australia.

Made in the USA
Middletown, DE
31 July 2020

14135638R00106